TAYLOR INSTITUTION LIBRARY

Treasures of the Taylorian

Series One: Reformation Pamphlets

Volume 4

Passional Christi und Antichristi
Antithesis figurata vitæ Christi et Antichristi

Passional of Christ and Antichrist
Antithesis of the Life of Christ and Antichrist
in Pictures

Edited by Edmund Wareham,
Ulrich Bubenheimer and Henrike Lähnemann

Taylor Institution Library, Oxford, 2021

Table of Contents

The Taylor Reformation Pamphlet Series

Henrike Lähnemann

Since their acquisition, the Reformation pamphlets have been one of the great teaching resources at the Taylor Institution Library, and Edmund Wareham has been instrumental in making sure that they have continued to be used as such for the most recent generations of students in both the Faculties of History and Modern Languages.

Edmund Wareham and a group of History of the Book students while setting up a Reformation pamphlet exhibition in the Voltaire Room of the Taylorian in 2016

The 'Passional Christi und Antichristi' is particularly suitable to spark discussions about the materiality of Reformation pamphlets, the significance of visual communication, polemics and propaganda, and the argumentative use of Scripture.

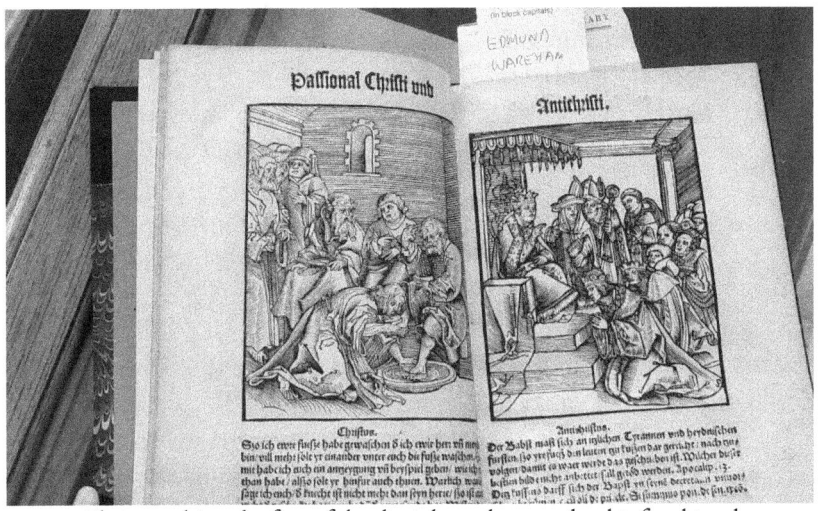

Christ washing the feet of the disciples – the pope has his feet kissed
Opening of the *Passional* chosen by Edmund Wareham for the exhibition in 2016

When we planned the series of the 'Treasures of the Taylorian. Series One: Reformation Pamphlets' for the Reformation quincentenary 2017, we started with a text which celebrated also an Oxford anniversary, the 'Sendbrief vom Dolmetschen', which had been on the syllabus since 1917 – and still works as a very effective way to introduce students to concepts of translation, historical linguistics, and early modern literature and culture. From the next year on we moved in chronological sequence, trailing the Reformation publication schedule by half a millennium, with the 'Sermon von Ablass und Gnade' in 2018 and the 'Von der Freiheit eines Christenmenschen' in 2020, and now catching up with the *Passional*, published in different editions in the course of summer 2021.

Simultaneously, we built up the website for additional student editions on https://editions.mml.ox.ac.uk/topics/reformation.shtml

Collaboration has been at the heart of the Reformation pamphlet project from the start, with many of the digital editions produced by a number of students; the *Passional* was first encoded by Natascha Domeisen as part of her History of the Book Master option in 2018, the Latin version was added by Eva Neufeind as part of a Digital Humanities internship in 2021. Not only would the whole enterprise not have been possible without Emma Huber's invaluable expertise (and patience!) in TEI encoding and meta-data, further colleagues have also helped in various ways: from the start, Howard Jones provided the linguistic expertise for the translations and the linguistic commentary; for the previous volumes, contributions came from theologians, historians and Germanists from Germany and the UK.

This edition now takes collaboration to a new international level, with a reach of which the editing collective behind the *Passional* could only have dreamt: The launch will happen in partnership with the Pitts Theology Library where both authors of the introduction have held Fellowships, with Ulrich Bubenheimer being the inaugural Richard C. Kessler Fellow in 2019/20, Edmund Wareham following in his wake in 2020/21. This allows the sharing of research expertise, translations, and exhibition concepts – a triumph of digital tools over travel restrictions in times of Covid.

Oxford, May 2021

Introduction

The introduction is meant as a propaedeutic guide for the edition that highlights the theological, philosophical, material, linguistic, and stylistic importance of this work.

For an open access version of these chapters cf. the online version https://editions.mml.ox.ac.uk/editions/passional

The Bodleian Library copy of the third edition Erfurt 1521, Tr. Luth. 13 (34) open at the page with the Bodleian Library stamp during a seminar in the Centre for the Study of the Book 2017

1. Edition – Translation

Edmund Wareham

In his preface to the ninth volume of the Weimar edition of Martin Luther's works, published in 1893, Paul Pietsch explained the reasoning behind the inclusion of illustrations of woodcuts and Luther manuscripts in the appendix: "Through this we do not want to make a sacrifice to the fashion for illustrations in our current age but rather want to follow an inner necessity. If the *Passional of Christ and Antichrist* is included in the works of Luther, which is done so with good reason, then the images have to be included because without them the text hovers in the air."[1] Gustav Kawerau provided an extensive introduction to his edition of the *Passional*, while the images, reproduced by the Stuttgart firm Martin Rommel & Co., were relegated to an appendix at the back of the book.[2] Some 128 years later the challenges of how best to reproduce the pamphlet both in print and also now increasingly in a digital format remain.[3]

This present works sets out from the premise that, while the woodcuts in the *Passional* produced by Lucas Cranach the Elder (1472–1553) have rightly been give the attention that they deserve,

---

[1] WA 9, 11: Zum ersten Male bringt unsere Ausgabe in diesem Bande als Beilagen Nachbildungen von Holzschnitten und von Lutherhandschriften. Wir wollen damit nicht der Illustrationsmode unsrer Zeit ein Opfer bringen, sondern folgen einer inneren Nothwendigkeit. Wenn einmal das Passional Christi und Antichristi den Werken Luthers eingereiht wurde, was ja mit gutem Grunde geschehen durfte (vgl. Kaweraus Einleitung), so konnten die Bilder, ohne die der Text in der Luft schwebt, nicht fehlen.

[2] WA 9, 677-700 (introduction by Kawerau), 701-715 (edition), 807-836 (images).

[3] See, for example, the British Library's digital photographs of the pamphlets which reproduce each page individually, rather than as a double spread: Luther's anti-papist pamphlet, Passional Christi und Antichristi, 1521. There are often conservation reasons behind the decision. The attribution of the pamphlet to Luther is misleading (see discussion below).

there is a danger that the texts which accompany them have become relegated and left hovering in the air. There is no doubt that the visual qualities of the pamphlet are what made it so striking and lay behind its success. Described by Robert Scribner as "the most successful work of visual propaganda produced by the Reformation"[4], there is consensus that the twenty-six woodcuts, thirteen of Christ and thirteen of the pope/Antichrist, gave the pamphlet its power and immediacy. Hans J. Hillerbrand has observed how "the text is sparse, limited, and expository. It rounds out and complements the message of the woodcuts, rather than vice versa."[5] He adds that "even devoid of their text, minimal as it is, the pictures convey their message."[6] Lyndal Roper and Jennifer Spinks have also recently argued that "Lutherans learnt to let images speak for themselves and when words were supplied, they were subordinated to images."[7] Even in our present day, the pamphlet can be readily used in the classroom or lecture theatre with pupils and students who have no access to Latin or German.[8]

While there is no doubt that the pamphlet could appeal to an illiterate audience, it would be reductive to limit our analysis purely to this one group in trying to understand how the ideas embodied within it

---

[4] Robert W. Scribner, *For the Sake of the Simple Folk. Popular Propaganda for the German Reformation* (Oxford: 1981, 1994), p. 149.

[5] Hans J. Hillerbrand, 'The Antichrist in the Early German Reformation: Reflections on Theology and Propaganda', in: *Germania Illustrata: Essays on Early Modern Germany Presented to Gerald Strauss*, ed. Andrew C. Fix and Susan Karant-Nunn (Kirksville, Mo.: Sixteenth Century Journal Publishers, 1992), pp. 3-17 (p. 8).

[6] Hillerbrand 1992, p. 9.

[7] Lyndal Roper and Jennifer Spinks, 'Karlstadt's *Wagen*: The First Visual Propaganda for the Reformation', *Art History* 40/2 (2017): 256-285 (p. 261).

[8] Extracts of the pamphlet are included, for example, in *Discovering the Western Past: A Look at the Evidence. Vol. II: Since 1500*, ed. Merry E. Wiesner-Hans, Julius R. Ruff and William Bruce Wheeler (Boston: Cengage Learning, ⁶2008), p. 319.

were transmitted and ultimately received.[9] Dating from May 1521, the bi-medial pamphlet the *Passional* is a striking example of what has been described as the "hybridisation" of media in this period, in which both text and image could work together to propagate Reformation ideas.[10] It is significant that on the title page of the Latin edition, the *Antithesis figurata*, four lines of verse are included which say explicitly: *Read this whoever is driven by love of true piety.*

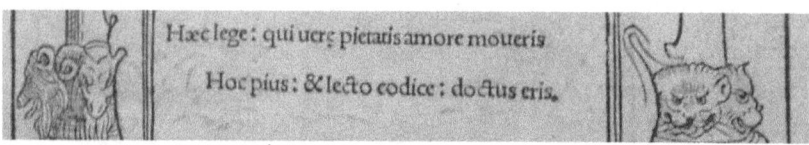

Hæc lege, qui veræ pietatis amore moveris.
From the title page of the Bodleian copy of the Antithesis, Douce C 313

The use of the verb *to read* suggests that the textual elements were in fact given precedence over the images or at the very least were recognised as significant.[11] Some pairs of images, such as the third pair in which Christ washes the feet of his disciples while the pope has his feet kissed, could be understood from the woodcuts alone. But in other pairs, such as the eleventh, the contrast between Christ and pope could only be understood from the texts, in which the inner

---

[9] Peter Kushner, 'Images for the simple; words for the wise. Cranach's and Melanchthon's Passional', *Skript Historisch Tijdschrift* 21.4 (2014): 277-302 (p. 290) noted if "scholarship [is] rich in knowing what Cranach intended to argue in the Passional we are poor when it comes to knowing what it meant to the people who might have read it."

[10] David Bagchi, 'Printing, Propaganda, and Public Opinion', in: *The Oxford Encyclopedia of Martin Luther*, ed. Derek R. Nelson and Paul R. Hinlicky, vol. 3 (Oxford: Oxford University Press, 2017), cols 187-209 (col. 190). This position is also expounded by Bobbi Dykema, *Luther, Cranach, and the Passional Christi und Antichristi* (Saarbrücken: OmniScriptum, 2017), pp. 28-29.

[11] Thomas Kaufmann, *Die Mitte der Reformation. Eine Studie zu Buchdruck und Publizistik im deutschen Sprachgebiet, zu ihren Akteuren und deren Strategien, Inszenierungs- und Ausdrucksformen* (Tübingen: Mohr Siebeck 2019), pp. 646-7, n. 863.

kingdom of God is contrasted with the outer kingdom of the Antichrist.

On one level the texts presented a clear contrast between Christ and pope, namely that of Bible versus canon law, or, in the interpretation of the author(s), truth versus falsehood. A closer analysis of the texts can refine this further. As Thomas Kaufmann has recently demonstrated, the texts underneath each woodcut, as well as on the title page and in the postscript, had distinct functions. Thus the Bible passages underneath the scenes of Christ's life gave these images their meaning. Underneath the first woodcut, for example, the quotation from John 6:15 (*When Jesus became aware that they were going to come and make him king, he escaped again to the mountain, he alone*) explains what is happening in the scene above. By contrast the visual representations of the pope derived their meaning through their opposition to those of Christ. The texts underneath the papal images – quotations from canon law, the Bible and statements by the author(s) – were only made plausible through the image and its opposition to Christ. In this way these texts had more of an affirmatory quality, confirming the message which was already present in the image.[12]

If the text as a whole has been downplayed in interpretations of the *Passional*, then it is particularly the case for the Latin printed edition, the *Antithesis of the Life of Christ and Antichrist in Pictures*. In his otherwise extremely extensive edition, Kawerau referred to the Latin text only rarely to clarify points in the German text. It is apparent that he regarded it as only of secondary importance.[13] Yet as Ulrich Bubenheimer demonstrates in the essay that follows, agreeing with Kaufmann, evidence suggests that the Latin text was written first, but only published after the completion of the German-language Wittenberg editions. Alongside the references to canon law which

---

[12] Kaufmann 2019, p. 670.
[13] Kaufmann 2019, p. 646, n. 863.

are given in their abbreviated Latin form, a number of different Latin phrases are retained in the main body of the German text (I 2: *Summa summarum*; VII 14: *animalia ventris*; X 19: *Vbi ist dan Patrimonium Petri*; Postscript: *famosus libellus*). This indicates that the translator(s) already had the Latin text before them. In addition, certain translation choices (see I 1) show that the translation was made from Latin into German and not vice versa. When Luther wrote to his friend Georg Spalatin (1484-1545), the secretary of the Elector Frederick the Wise (1463-1525), on 7 March 1521, he declared, that at this moment an *Antithesis figurata Christi et papæ* was being prepared which would be good for the laity.[14] The title of the work is so similar to the one that was eventually published that we can assume he had the Latin work before him and that he saw great promise in the anti-Papal visual polemic for lay and unlearned people. The final statement may also indicate that he was already aware that a vernacular version was being produced.[15]

Until now there has been neither a critical edition of the *Antithesis figurata* nor a recognition that the Latin text has survived in two printing variants. The printer initially delivered an edition (A) that contained several printing errors, as evidenced by the copy held in the Bodleian Library, Douce C 313 [VD16 L 5589; Benzing/Claus no. 1024]. For the later print run (B) the typesetting was not completely redone but four corrections were made to the text.[16] Of

---

[14] WA.B 2, 283, 24-25 (no. 385), see below the introduction of Bubenheimer §6.

[15] Kaufmann 2019, pp. 647-648.

[16] See below Bubenheimer §2. Benzing/Claus (vol. 2, p. 95) also list for no. 1024 a supposed print variant which contains the correction *ANTI-CHRISTI* (instead of *ANTICHRISTI*) on the second line of the title page. But the copy used as evidence in the Staats- und Universitätsbibliothek Göttingen: 8 TH TH II, 207/7 (1) RARA does not contain a print variant. The difference in the title is the result of an erasure and a subsequent handwritten correction. The error can be traced back to Helmut Kind, *Die Lutherdrucke des 16. Jahrhunderts und die Lutherhandschriften der Niedersächsischen Staats- und Universitätsbibliothek Göttingen* (Göttingen: 1967), no. 530c. L 5590, which lists the supposed variant as separate print run, should be removed.

the fourteen copies which are known to exist of both variants of the Latin edition, many show active signs of use, including coloured-in woodcuts[17] and handwritten annotations.[18]

An edition is crucial for understanding the process of compilation. Not only can clear typographical errors be corrected, but it is possible to trace how the author(s) made use of the Bible and canon law and where they differed from it, sometimes it seems even purposefully. In VII 14, for example, in the text about replacement preachers for bishops, the positive attribution of such men as *idoneos* (suitable) was removed, despite it being found in the original decretal.[19] In this way the extract from the decretal, itself presented completely out of its original context, was amended in a small but significant way to heighten the contrast between Christ, who preaches the kingdom of God, and the pope and clergy, who neglect their preaching duties.

---

[17] Österreichische Nationalbibliothek Wien: 31.W.71 ALT PRUNK; Universitäts-bibliothek Heidelberg: Sal. 121,29 RES. The latter also contains handwritten annotations.

[18] Staats- und Stadtbibliothek Augsburg: 4 Th 131 contains two-line hexameters to accompany every image. Other copies, with the edition listed where known: Universitäts- und Landesbibliothek Sachsen-Anhalt, Halle: Ib 4187 a (30) (variant A); Thüringer Universitäts- und Landesbibliothek Jena: 4 Op.theol.V,3(12), sigs. A1r-A2v (fols. 317r-318v) (variant B); four copies in the Herzog August Bibliothek Wolfenbüttel: A: 98.11 Theol. (17); H: S 41.4° Helmst. (5); H: S 41.4o; M: Li 6119; Ratsschulbibliothek Zwickau.

[19] Decretal., I 31 De officio iudicis ordinarii c. 15 Inter ceterea, CorpIC 2, 192: *Unde, quum saepe cotingat, quod episcopi propter suas occupationes multiplices, vel invaletudines corporales, aut hostiles incursus, seu occasiones alias, ne dicamus defectum scientiae, quod in eis reprobandum est omnino, nec de cetero tolerandum, per se ipsos non sufficiunt ministrare populo verbum Dei, maxime per amplas dioeceses et diffusas: generali constitutione sancimus, ut episcopi viros idoneos ad sanctae praedicationis officium salubriter exsequendum assumant, potentes in opere et sermone, qui plebes sibi commissas vice ipsorum, quum per se iidem nequiverint, sollicite visitantes, eas verbo aedificent et exemplo, quibus ipsi, quum indiguerint, congrue necessaria subministrent, ne pro necessariorum defectu compellantur desistere ab incepto.*

Paying closer attention to the *Antithesis figurata* can also allow a systematic comparison between the Latin and German versions to understand how the translation was undertaken. For the most part, the German text offers a shortened version of the Latin. There were primarily technological considerations behind this decision, given that the typeface for German was larger than for Latin and that the number of letters required for a direct translation into German was in fact longer.[20] In VII 14 again, for instance, the long list of reasons given for absentee bishops, which can be found in the Latin, is simply removed from the German. Yet the translation process was not merely an act of shortening. While in IV 8 the *Antithesis figurata* quotes from canon law directly, the *Passional* in fact adds significant extra information, notably that the pope orders the ban or interdict on those who levy tax on clerical persons or their property.

In this way, the *Passional* cannot simply be regarded as a translation of the *Antithesis*, but rather as an active process of engagement, adaptation and refinement, in itself reflective of the transmission history of the pamphlet as a whole. A picture emerges of the author(s) and compiler(s) constantly seeking to modify and in many respects clarify the message of the pamphlet. Some of these changes were visual. The first two Wittenberg editions of the *Passional*, for example, featured a woodcut of Christ going on foot, which was subsequently replaced by an image of Christ carrying the cross (VI 11B) in order to heighten the contrast with the woodcut of the pope being carried. Other changes were textual. In the two Strasbourg editions, printed in 1521, two new extra sets of contrasts were added, as well as a new elaborate title page with dialogue, verse couplets in both German and Latin and an expanded postscript. Some phrases in the German text underneath each woodcut were also changed for

---

[20] Howard Jones, 'The German and Latin Versions', in: Martin Luther, *Von der Frei-heit eines Christenmenschen / On the Freedom of a Christian*, ed. Howard Jones and Henrike Lähnemann (Oxford: Taylor Institution Library 2020), pp. lxxii-xc (p. lxxii) who notes how German generally has a higher word-count than Latin.

reasons of clarification and emphasis. This publication argues that scholarship must not simply draw conclusions from the Wittenberg German edition of the *Passional*, but rather take into greater account both the transmission history of the various editions and the many different textual elements of which they consisted.

While the question of who prepared the translation of the *Antithesis figurata* into German remains uncertain, assertions in recent literature that Luther wrote the German descriptions are wide off the mark.[21] Instead, as Bubenheimer argues in his essay, the evidence shows that both Philip Melanchthon (1497-1560) and the jurist Johannes Schwertfeger (c. 1488-1524) were involved in the composition of both the *Antithesis figurata* and *Passional* and that Schwertfeger may have even played a more leading role than has previously been recognised. We can no longer assume that he merely provided the references to canon law to the antitheses which had been developed by Melanchthon, a claim often repeated in the literature without basis.

A focus on the texts can finally allow us to trace the significance of the pamphlet in new ways. In his wonderfully rich essay, Scribner traced the extensive influence which the *Passional* had on later works of visual propaganda.[22] Yet the different editions of both the *Passional* and the *Antithesis figurata* were also influential textually. Most immediately, in 1523, Heinrich von Kettenbach, a former Franciscan friar who abandoned the monastic life for Lutheranism, published a set of 66 contrasts between Christ and the papal Antichrist in a pamphlet devoid of illustrations but which built on many of the oppositions already present in the *Passional*.[23] The English Protestant

---

[21] David M. Whitford, 'The Papal Antichrist: Martin Luther and the Underappreciated Influence of Lorenzo Valla', *Renaissance Quarterly* 61/1 (2008): 26-52 (p. 42).

[22] Scribner, *Propaganda*, p. 157.

[23] Heinrich von Kettenbach, *Vergleychung* || *des allerheyli=||gisten herren/|| vnd vatter des Bapsts/ gegen || dem seltzamen frembdẽ gast yñ || der Christenheyt/ gnant Jesus/||*

John Frith (1503-1533) made use of Kettenbach's work and the *Passional* in his 1529 publication *Antithesis of Christes Acts*, just one example of the international reception of the pamphlet.[24] The explicit use of the word *Antithesis* in the title would suggest to me that Frith had access to or was aware of the *Antithesis figurata*, as well as the *Passional*. Musically the number of songs referring to the Antichrist and the apocalypse also reached a peak during the early 1520s.[25] In 1523, *A New Song of the Antichrist in Rome and his Apostles* was published in Würzburg which referred explicitly to the *same Antichrist who with his companions is completely against Christ. Whatever he has taught us do, do the complete opposite of it.*[26]

Different aspects of the text also proved influential long after its original appearance in 1521. In 1563, for example, Christoph Marstaller, a Lutheran pastor in Schwäbisch Hall, published a text on death and the last judgement.[27] The first chapter warned of the world

---

der ynn kurtzer zeyt widderumb || *ynn Teutsch landt ist komen/*|| *vnd yetzund widder will ynn* || *Egypten landt/ als eyn* || *verachter bey vns.*|| ... *Bruder Heinrich kettenbach.*|| (Wittenberg: 1523) [VD16 K 836].

[24] *A pistle to the Christen reader* || *The Revelation of Antichrist.*|| *Antithesis/ wherin are compa*||*red to geder Christes actes* || *and oure holye father* || *the Popes.*|| (Antwerp: 1529) [VD16 ZV 26131]. See Catherine Dejeumont and William Kemp, 'John Frith's Antithesis of Christes Actes compared to the Popes (1529) in relation to Heinrich von Kettenbachs Vergleychung', *Reformation* 12/1 (2007): 33-68.

[25] Rebecca Wagner Oettinger, *Music as Propaganda in the German Reformation* (Aldershot: Ashgate, 2001), pp. 171-201.

[26] *Ein neus lied vom Anti*||*christ zu Rom vnd seinen* || *Aposteln/ wie sie vns/ durch verschuldung* || *vnser sunden vnd vndanckbarkeyt gegen* || *got/ verfureth haben mit iren lehren* || *gesetzen/ vnd gepoten/ dorin ver*||*mant werden alle Christen* || *solche verfurische lehr* || *zu verlassen* || *vnd die Euangelisch warheit* || *anzunemen.*|| ... || (Würzburg: 1523) [VD16 N 1237], fol. A1v-A2r: *Hernach wil ich in nenen / den selben Antichrist welcher mit seyn gesellen / stracks wider Chirstum ist / was er vns hat geleret / thut diser gantz vmbkeren.*

[27] Christoph Marstaller, *Der Welt vrlaub von den Menschen Kindern Vnd Wie der Jüngste Tag vor der Thür / nach ausweisung der wort Christi / auch deren Zeichen / so Christus vor seiner andern Zukunfft vermeldet / Allen fromen Christen dieser letzten Zeit*

being full of false prophets who will claim that what they say is the word of God. In the chapter Marstaller quotes a *little verse* (*Verslein*) which demonstrates that the actions and deeds of the pope are against Christ and his apostles.[28] The verse is in fact the rhyming German couplets and Latin hexameters which are included in the second Strasbourg edition of the *Passional*, published by Johann Knobloch the Elder.[29] Marstaller presents them in a long list, providing the Latin hexameter followed by the German couplet, with biblical references in the margin. The work is not illustrated. Following the quotation of the fifteen pairs, Marstaller explains that *no one should accuse me of recording such things based on my own head or partiality, since everything which is presented here of our dear Lord Christ can be found in the Gospels and the decretals of the pope. From this we can easily deduce who is the Antichrist, opposed to our Lord Christ.*[30] Marstaller was indeed not quoting from his own head, but rather seems to have had access to the second Strasbourg edition of the *Passional*. Significantly, he was drawn to the verses which appeared above and alongside the woodcuts, in both German and Latin, and transmitted them in a new time and context in which engagement with the papal Antichrist had

---

zur warnung / vnd ires Lebens besserung (Oberursel: 1563) [VD16 M 1137]. On the VD16 database five works are listed as being authored by Marstaller between 1563 and 1575. In addition there is a reference to him as a witness in a case from 22 April 1562 (Landesarchiv Baden-Württemberg, Abt. Staatsarchiv Ludwigsburg, B 113 I U 948).

[28] Marstaller 1563, fols. C6r–C6v.
[29] *Passional Christi vnd Antichristi. || Christus | Petre/ | wa[n] würd | entbunde[n] ich?* [Strasbourg: Johann Knobloch d. Ä. 1521?]. Benzing/Claus no. 1019 [VD16 L 5582]. Bodleian Library Oxford: Tr. Luth. 250a. That Marstaller made use of this edition, and not the first Strasbourg edition of Johann Prüss the Younger [VD16 L 5583] can be shown by him quoting the Latin verse *Regna fugit Christus / præsulque suscipit urbis.* Prüss's edition reads *Regna fugit Christus / Præsulque Papa imperat orbi.*
[30] Marstaller 1563, fol. C7v: *Niemand sol mir zumessen / das ich solchs hie aus meinem eigen kopff oder mutwillen auffzeichne / denn alles was jetzt angezeigt / von vnserm lieben Herren Christo findestu in den Euangelii vnd Decreten des Bapsts / daraus wir vns leichtlich zuberichten / wer der Antichrist / so vnserm Herrn Christo zu wider ist / sey.*

re-emerged.[31] It is hoped that this present work can stimulate future such work into the reception history of the pamphlet.

While extracts of the *Passional* have been translated before, they are often relegated to a footnote, and translations of the whole pamphlet often merge the Latin and German versions together without explanation.[32] Alongside the critical edition of the *Antithesis figurata*, the present publication also presents an English translation of the Latin text. In addition, it offers a diplomatic transcription and translation of the third edition of the *Passional* from the workshop of the Erfurt printer Matthäus Males, dating from 1521. A copy of this is held in the Taylor Institution Library, Oxford, ARCH.8°.G. 1521(19). Except for the addition of his own title page, the third edition imitated every detail of the Wittenberg editions, including typographical errors. Finally, it offers a diplomatic transcription of all the additional text (title page, verses, new sets of contrasts, postscript) in the second Strasbourg edition of the *Passional*, printed by Johann Knobloch the Elder in 1521 and based on the copy held in Oxford, Bodleian Library Tr. Luth. 250a. I provide English translations for all the new text. For each image I provide a systematic comparison of the Latin texts with the different German versions.

---

[31] See, for example, *ANTITHESIS.|| Das ist || Kurtze beschrei=||bung/ Christi vnd des || Antichrists/ Darin jr beider || Art/ lehr/ vnd thaten gegen||einander werden ge=||hal-ten.|| Jn deutscher sprach zu=||uoren also nie außgangen* (Heidelberg: 1563) [VD16 R 3101]. This was a German translation/adaptation of *Antithesis de praeclaris Christi et indignis Papæ facinoribus, cum Dei decalogis mandatis Antichristi oppositis, cumq[ue] vtri-usq[ue] morū descriptione: quemadmodum sancta Scriptura tradit. modio, sed vt in can-delabro* (Geneva: 1557) by Simon Du Rosier (Rosarius). Further research is needed to establish the links between these texts and the *Passional/Antithesis figurata*.

[32] Gerald Fleming, 'On the Origin of the Passional Christi und Antichristi and Lucas Cranach the Elder's Contribution to Reformation Polemics in the Iconography of the Passional', *Gutenberg-Jahrbuch* (1973): 351-368; Dejeumont and Kemp 2007; Dykema, *Luther*, pp. 36-89; images from a seminar website Bangor 2000.

Lucas Cranach, working in conjunction with the Wittenberg theology professor Andreas Bodenstein von Karlstadt (1486-1541), had produced the first piece of visual propaganda for the Reformation, the broadsheet *Fuhrwagen* (January-March 1519). As with the *Antithesis figurata* and *Passional* it was based around opposition: two wagons advance in opposite directions. The upper wagon moves towards Christ, while the lower one towards hell. It was also produced first in Latin and then in German,[33] with similar concerns about the latter taking up too much space. But it failed spectacularly to grasp what could and could not be conveyed visually.[34] While the *Fuhrwagen* overwhelms the reader with its mass of texts scattered across the broadsheet, the *Antithesis figurata* and *Passional* demonstrate a new-found confidence, assurance and awareness of how text and image could be combined most effectively. It was no wonder that Luther on 26 May 1521, now in the Wartburg castle after his interdict at the Diet of Worms, declared that *The antithetical Passional pleases me greatly.*[35]

---

[33] Both versions have been edited by Alejandro Zorzin in: *Kritische Gesamtausgabe der Schriften und Briefe Andreas Bodensteins von Karlstadt*, ed. Thomas Kaufmann, vol. II (Heidelberg: Verein für Reformationsgeschichte, 2019), pp. 121-134 and 179-194, together with illustrations at the end of the volume, figs. 3-5.

[34] Roper and Spinks 2017, p. 256.

[35] That Luther seemed to be combining both the German and Latin titles, provides further evidence of why we must place the different editions of the pamphlet in closer dialogue with each other. Cf. below the essay by Bubenheimer §6.

The *Fuhrwagen* by Andreas Karlstadt and Lucas Cranach of 1519
size: 29,8x40,5 (ca. A3)
(Deutsches Historisches Museum, Gr 53/1)

2. Content – Sources – Author – Reception

Ulrich Bubenheimer, translated by Edmund Wareham

1. Structure and Content

In spring 1521 a comparison between Christ and the Antichrist/pope, combining image and text, appeared in Wittenberg. It was published anonymously in both a Latin version (*Antithesis of the Life of Christ and Antichrist in Pictures – Antithesis figurata vitæ Christi et Antichristi*) and a German one (*Passional of Christ and Antichrist – Passional Christi und Antichristi*). None of those involved in its production, the deviser of the picture series, artist, authors, translator and the printer, divulged their names. This polemical satire of the papacy consisted of thirteen antitheses or contrasts in the Wittenberg version, numbered below with Roman numerals (I-XIII). Each antithesis consisted of two woodcuts: on each double page there is a scene from the life of Christ on the left and a scene from the life of the pope on the right. A text of variable length is included under each of the twenty-six woodcuts (numbered with Arabic numerals 1-26) and provides a commentary.[1] An additional woodcut on the title page provides a decorative border in a Renaissance style for the *Passional* and the *Antithesis* which has no bearing on the content of the pamphlets.[2]

An overview of the structure of the sequence of images and themes depicted in the woodcuts is presented below (Table 1). Sources from

---

[1] The German version of the text is edited in WA 9, 701-15 with a detailed introduction by Gustav Kawerau (WA 9, 677-700). The woodcuts are reproduced in the appendix of WA 9 as addenda.

[2] Reproduced in Johannes Luther, *Die Titeleinfassungen der Reformationszeit*. Mit Verbesserungen und Ergänzungen von Josef Benzing, Helmut Claus und Martin von Hase (Hildesheim; New York: Georg Olms, 1973), plate 6; description of the titlepage in Dieter Koepplin, Tilmann Falk, *Lukas Cranach. Gemälde, Zeichnungen, Druckgraphik* (Basel; Stuttgart: Birkhäuser, 1976), vol. 2, pp. 586, 588.

the Bible and canon law[3] for the themes of the thirteen antitheses with each of their two images are given. The biblical quotations usually appear under the scenes of Christ and sometimes under individual scenes of the pope, while quotations from canon law are only added to the papal scenes. As several Bible passages are often quoted under each woodcut, the Bible passage from which each Christ scene (and in two cases the Antichrist scene) has been developed is highlighted in bold. As a general rule the texts under the scenes of Christ are made up of Bible passages; only in a few cases are additional comments added. Under most of the scenes of the pope, critical comments against the papacy are included by the author(s), in addition to the quotations from canon law and the Bible.

Table 1: Image Themes and Quotations

I The Kingdom
    1. Christ flees from the offer of a royal crown: **John 6:15;** John 18:36; Luke 22:25–26
    2. The pope with a crown (tiara) receives knights with cannons and mercenaries: 2 Pet 2:1; 10; *Clem.,* De sententia et re iudicata II 11 c. Pastoralis

II The Crown
    3. Christ is crowned with thorns: **John 19:2**
    4. The pope is crowned with a tiara: *Decr.,* d. 96 c. 13 Constantinus

III Washing or Kissing the Feet
    5. Christ washes and kisses the feet of the disciples: **John 13:14–17;** Rev 13:15
    6. The pope has his feet kissed: *Decretal.,* V 33 De privilegiis c. 12 Cum olim; *Clem.,* I 10 De sententia excommunicationis c. 4 Si summus pontifex

---

[3] I have relied for the most part on the edition in WA 9 for the evidence of the sources quoted from canon law. I have added any missing information. For the full information on the sources cf. the edition below.

IV Paying Tax
   7. Christ and Peter pay customs: **Matt 17:23–26**; Rom 13:(4), 7[4]
   8. The pope imposes the ban on authorities who tax the clergy: *Lib. Sextus*, III 23 De immunitate ecclesiarum C. 1

V Caring for the Poor and Powerful
   9. Christ in prayer with the lame, lepers and blind: Phil 2:6-8
   10. The pope gloats over a knight's tournament: *Decr.*, d. 86 c. 4 Quando[5] with gloss[6]

VI Carrying the Cross and the Palanquin
   11A.[7] Christ goes by foot: John 4:6; Matt 16:24
   11B. Christ bears his cross: John 4:6; Matt 16:24; **John 19:17**
   12. The pope is carried on a palanquin: *Decr.*, [C. 17 q. 4][8] c. 29 Si quis suadente diabolo

VII Preaching and Feasting
   13. Christ preaches to the people: **Luke 4:43–44**
   14. The pope at a feast: Isa 56:12 with Titus 1:12; *Decretal.*, I 31 De officio iudicis ordinarii c. 15 Inter cetera

---

[4] *Antithesis* quotes Rom 13:7, the *Passional* extends the quotation freely according to Rom 13:4.

[5] CorpIC 1, 298: *Quando necessitas discipline in moribus coercendis dicere vos dura verba compellit: si etiam ipsi modum vos excesisse sentitis non a vobis exigitur: ut vos a subditis veniam postuletis: ne apud eos quos oportet esse subiectos: dum nimium servatur humilitas regendi* **frangatur auctoritas** (author's emphasis in bold).

[6] The gloss of frangatur auctoritas quoted in the footnote above reads as follows: **Frangatur auctoritas.** *Augere enim ex ingenio debet dignitatem. Nimia enim familiaritas contemptum generat [...] quod verum est inter fatuos: [...] illa ergo auctoritas vade prius reconciliari fratri tuo antequam offeras ad altare: de prelatis non intelligitur. Decretum Gratiani [...]*, Lyon: Nicolaus de Benedictis, 12 May 1506, fol. 87rb (author's emphasis in bold).

[7] Two different scenes of Christ exist for this antithesis. Scene A (only in the first two Wittenberg editions of the *Passional*, Benzing/Claus no. 1015 and 1014) shows Jesus barefoot on his way with two disciples. Scene B (in the Wittenberg editions Benzing/Claus no. 1016, 1017 and 1024, as well as in the Erfurt and Strasbourg editions) show the motive of Christ bearing the cross.

[8] In the text the references to *Causa* and *questio* are missing.

VIII Low and High Status

15. Birth of Christ in the stable: Luke 9:58; 2 Cor 8:9

16. The pope with tiara and knight's armour wages war: *Decr.*, C. 15 q. 6 c. 2 Auctoritatem; *Decr.*, C. 23 q. 5 c. 46 Omnium; *Decr.*, C. 23 q. 8 c. 9 Omni

IX Humility and Pride

17. Entry into Jerusalem: Christ rides on a donkey, accompanied by the simple folk: **Matt 21:1-8.** John 12:14-15.

18. Exit into hell: the pope rides on a horse, accompanied by mercenaries and the high clergy: *Decr.*, C. 12 q. 1 c. 7 duo; *Decr.*, d. 96 c. 14 Constantinus; *Extrav. com.*[9], I 1 c. 1 Super gentes

X Poverty and Wealth

19. Sending out of the disciples: Christ demands poverty of them: **Matt 10:9-10;** Acts 3:6

20. The pope shows a bishop a castle: *Decr.*, d. 80 c. 3 Episcopi; *Decr.*, d. 70 c. 2 Sanctorum

XI Internal and External Kingdoms[10]

21. The disciples do not wash their hands before the meal – Christ above in argument with the Pharisees: Luke 17:20-21; **Matt 15:1-3;** Is 29:13

22. The pope is worshipped by the clergy and people: 1 Tim 4:1, 3

XII Rejecting or Collecting Money

23. Christ drives out the money changers from the temple: **John 2:14-16;** Matt 10:8; Acts 8:20

24. The pope sits in church, selling sealed letters: **2 Thess 2:4;** Dan 11:36-37; *Decr.*, d. 19 c. 2 Sic omnis; *Decr.*, C. 17 q. 4 c. 30 Nemini

XIII The End: Ascent or Descent

25. Ascension of Christ to heaven: John 12:26; **Rev 19:20-21;** 2 Thess 2:8

26. Descent of the pope into hell: **Act 1:9, 11;** Luke 1: 33

In view of the relationship of the images to the quoted sources in the texts we can establish the following: only one of the motives of

---

[9] In the text erroneously ascribed to the *Extravagentes Johannis XXII.*

[10] The antithesis between the internal and the external kingdom can only be deduced from the texts in this instance.

Christ, the birth of Christ in the stable (VIII 15), is not based on a quoted Bible passage. The motives of the Antichrist / papal scenes are the antitype of the scenes represented by Christ. In four cases Bible passages are quoted underneath images of the Antichrist (I 2; III 6; XII 24; XIII 26). These either contain warnings by the pseudo-prophets (1 Pet 2:1,10 in I 2) or introduce figures of biblical apocalypticism. They are then applied to the pope. Apocalyptic motives from the Bible also influence the last two images of the pope (XII 24; XIII 26). But for the most part the texts under the papal images include quotations from canon law, i.e. the *Decretum Gratiani*, and the papal decrees. The opposition of texts from the Bible and canon law forms one of the overarching antitheses of the pamphlet as a whole: Bible against canon law, or, according to the authors' interpretation, truth against falsehood.

2. Latin *Antithesis* and German *Passional* – First Edition and Sequence of Wittenberg Editions

Martin Luther referred for the first time to an illustrated antithesis in a letter written on 7 March 1521 to his friend Georg Spalatin (1484-1545), the secretary of the Elector Frederick the Wise (1463-1525): *At the moment an Antithesis of Christ and the pope is being prepared in images, a good book for the laity. (Iam paratur Antithesis figurata Christi et pap(a)e, bonus pro laicis liber).*[11] The name chosen by Luther for the work which was being prepared – *Antithesis figurata Christi et papæ* – is so close the title of the Latin edition (*Antithesis figurata vitæ Christi et Antichristi*) that we can assume that the version with Latin texts could have been the original. A translation of the texts for a German edition could only be completed in a second step. In order to clarify the question which version came first, I have compared the Latin text (*Antithesis figurata*) with the German version (*Passional*).

---

[11] WA.B 2, 283, 24-25 (no. 385).

The comparison is based on the following Wittenberg editions:

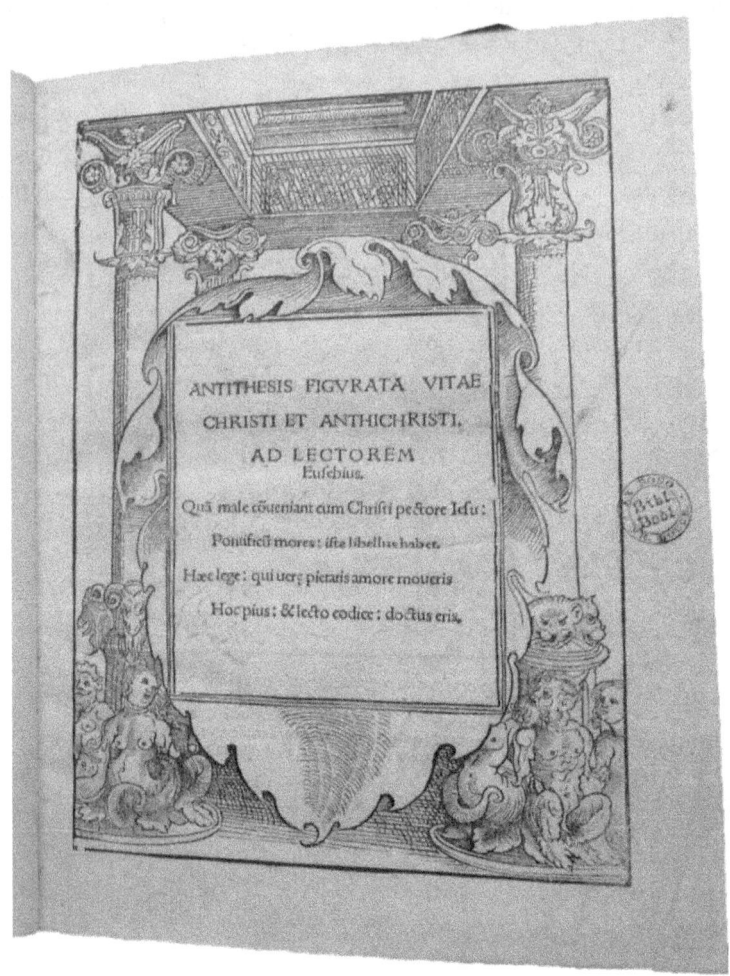

1. ANTITHESIS FIGVRATA VITÆ | CHRISTI ET ANTHICHRISTI. | AD
LECTOREM | Eusebius. ‖ Qua[m] male co[n]ueniant cum Christi pectore Iesu: |
[…]. [Wittenberg: Johann Grunenberg, 1521].[12] (Bodleian Library, Douce C 313)

---

[12] VD16 L 5589. Benzing/Claus no. 1024. I used the following copies: Bodleian
Library Oxford: Douce C 313; Universitätsbibliothek Heidelberg: Sal. 121,29 RES

2. Passional Christi vnd | Antichristi. [Wittenberg: Johann Grunenberg, 1521].[13]

The comparison reveals that the German text is a shortened version of the Latin. In the German text some isolated Latin formulations can be found which could not be comprehensible to readers without knowledge of Latin. X 19 provides the most striking example:

X 19: S. Petrus dixit: Aurum et argentum non habeo. Actuum. iii. Vbi est ergo patrimonium Petri? (*Antithesis figurata*, C2v)

(Saint Peter says: "I have neither gold nor silver." Acts 3. Where is therefore the inheritance of Peter?)

In the Wittenberg first edition of the German *Passional* the following version is transmitted:

X 19: Sanct Peter sagt/ Ich habe wyder golt nach silber act. 3. Vbi ist dan Patrimonium Petri? (*Passional,* fol. C2v).

The mixture of German and Latin in the second sentence is a clear sign that the text of the *Antithesis figurata* lay before the translator. While the quoted version of the German text was retained in all of

---

(containing handwritten annotations in Latin and coloured-in woodcuts, except for the title page); Staats- und Universitätsbibliothek Göttingen: 8 Th Th II 202/7_1 RARA. Benzing/Claus (vol. 2, p. 95) also list for no. 1024, a supposed print variant which contains the correction *ANTI-CHRISTI* (instead of *ANTHICHRISTI*) on the second line of the title page. But the copy used as evidence in the Staats- und Universitätsbibliothek Göttingen: 8 TH TH II, 207/7 (1) RARA does not contain a print variant. Rather the difference in the title is the result of an erasure and a subsequent handwritten correction. This error can be traced back to Helmut Kind, *Die Lutherdrucke des 16. Jahrhunderts und die Lutherhandschriften der Niedersächsischen Staats- und Universitätsbibliothek Göttingen* (Göttingen: Vandenhoeck & Ruprecht, 1967), no. 530c. As a result VD16 L 5590, in which the supposed variant is listed as its own edition, should be removed.

[13] First edition of the *Passional*: Benzing/Claus no. 1015 (not 1014!); VD16 L 5585. Copy of the Herzog August Bibliothek Wolfenbüttel: A: 116.5 theol. (18). No copies in Oxford.

the Wittenberg and Erfurt editions, in the Strasbourg edition, which on the whole offers an altered and expanded version of the pamphlet, the linguistic contrast is further heightened:

> X 19: Sanct Peter sagt/ Ich habe weder golt noch silber. Act.3.
> Wo ist dann Patrimonium vnd erbgůt[14] Petri.[15]

Alongside the use of Latin words in the German texts, the repeated shortening of the texts in the German version indicates the precedence of the Latin version.

The reduction in length was as a result of the technological challenges of printing. The space under the woodcuts available for text was limited. As the number of letters for the completed translated German text would have been longer and the typeface for German was larger than the Latin, the priority was to shorten the quotations from canon law and, to a lesser extent, the biblical quotations.[16] It is therefore necessary to turn to the Latin version to interpret the texts. Previous research, however, had not recognised that the Latin text has survived in two printing variants. First, the printer had delivered an edition (A) that contained several printing errors.[17] This was

---

[14] The Latin word *Patrimonium* is indeed retained, but translated by *erbgůt*.

[15] *Passional Christi vnd Antichristi* [Strasbourg: Johann Prüss, 1521], fol. C2v. Benzing/Claus no. 1018; VD16 L 5583. Copy of the Universitätsbibliothek Heidelberg: Q 3361-4 (contemporary ownership mark: *Joannis Beckij Vberling.[ensis]*, i.e. Johannes Beck from Überlingen). This print is the first of the two Strasbourg editions.

[16] The shortening of the quotations from canon law in the *Passional* (Wittenberg), fol. C1r for picture VIII 16 are particularly extensive. Here the Latin text was already so long that the first line was squeezed up against the lower edge of the woodcut and many abbreviations were used.

[17] The following copies belong to edition A: Staats- und Stadtbibliothek Augsburg: 4 Th 131; Bodleian Library Oxford: Douce C 313; Universitätsbibliothek Halle: Ib 4187a; Universitätsbibliothek Heidelberg: Sal. 121,29 RES.

followed by an edition (B) in which four improvements were made[18] without any other changes to the typesetting.[19]

The evidence that the German text is a translation of the Latin does not, however, mean that the Latin text was printed first.[20] Rather the Latin text was printed after the completion of the German-language Wittenberg editions. The sequence in which the German and the Latin editions in the workshop of Johann Grunenberg were produced can be established from the condition of the twenty-six plates used for printing the images. Over the course of the printing process, wear increased on the printing plates and this is clearly visible from the several traces of damage (tears and breaks) in the outer borders of the woodcuts.[21]

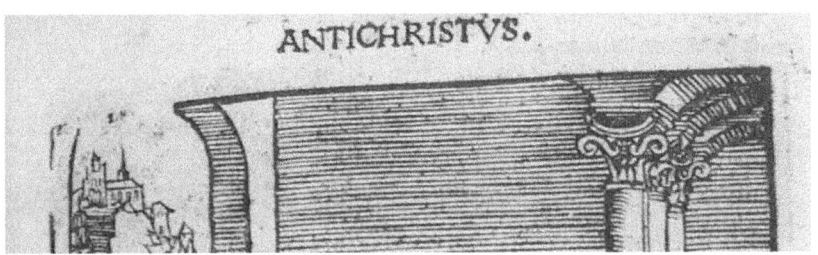

Broken top left edge on C3r of the *Antithesis* copy Bodleian Douce C 313

---

[18] Antithesis figurata, fol. A1v, l. 1, *raperetur* was improved to *raperent*; fol. A2r *vocante* (l. 2) was replaced by *vacante* and *Cesares* (l. 5) by *Caesares*; fol. C 6v, l. 1 *secrimina* was improved by insertion of a space into *se crimina*.

[19] The following copies belong to edition B: Universitätsbibliothek Göttingen: 8 Th Th II 202/7_1 RARA; Universitäts- und Landesbibliothek Jena: 4 Op. theol. V, 3.

[20] Thomas Kaufmann, *Neues von „Junker Jörg". Lukas Cranachs frühreformatorische Druckgraphik. Beobachtungen, Anfragen, Thesen und Korrekturen*, s. l. et a. (Weimar: Herzogin Anna Amalia Bibliothek, 2021), p. 59, n. 32, also reaches this conclusion.

[21] According to this criterium the following sequence of the Wittenberg editions can be reconstructed: The first edition was Benzing/Claus no. 1015. After this follow Benzing/Claus no. 1014, 1016 and 1017. Finally, the Latin text was printed (cf. *ibid.*, no. 1024.)

From this precedence of the Latin text it follows that the term *Passional* was not actually used in the Latin edition, but rather that the sequence of images was labelled as an *Antithesis of the Life of Christ and Antichrist*. The chosen scenes are in fact not just selected from the biblical tradition of the Passion of Christ but offer a selection of scenes from his entire life. Only a small number of these can actually be found in the iconographical tradition of the Passion of Christ.[22] This decision not simply to select motives limited to Christ's Passion can be explained by the aim of the images to contrast the behaviour of Christ with that of the Antichrist. A corresponding emphasis is also presented to the reader in the epigram printed on the titlepage which can only be found in the Latin version:

AD LECTOREM Eusebius.
Quam male conueniant cum Christi pectore Iesu:
Pontificum mores: iste libellus habet.
Hæc lege: qui veræ pietatis amore moueris
Hoc pius: et lecto codice: doctus eris. (A1r)

(Eusebius to the reader: How badly the customs of the popes conform with the spirit of Jesus Christ can be shown by this little book. Read this whoever is driven by love of true piety. When you have read this volume, you will be pious and learned.)

By placing the customs of the pope in opposition to the spirit of Christ, the poem formulates implicitly an antithesis of outer and inner which runs through the whole work. The life of the pope is characterised by spiritless externalisations, the life of Christ by the spirit of God. The third and fourth lines of the poem are intended to encourage people to read (and of course buy) the book. By reading this volume, it is promised, the reader will be made pious and learned.

---

[22] Cf. Wolfgang Braunfels; Michael Nitz, 'Leben Jesu', in: *Lexikon der christlichen Ikonographie,* ed. Engelbert Kirschbaum, vol. 3 (Freiburg im Breisgau: Herder, 1971), cols 39-85, especially cols 68-79.

The original version of the series of woodcuts contains only three scenes which traditionally belong to the inventory of the Passion of Christ: crown of thorns (II 3), washing of the feet (III 5), entry into Jerusalem (IX 17); the Ascension to heaven (XIII 25) could potentially be added to that list. A whole series of central motives which would normally be found in a Passional of Christ are missing, including the Agony in the Garden, arrest, carrying the cross and crucifixion. This absence of Passion scenes was somewhat reduced retrospectively. From the third German edition[23] the scene of Christ was swapped in the sixth contrast: Christ going by foot until overcome by fatigue (VI 11A) was replaced with Christ carrying the cross (VI 11B).[24] This also sharpened the antithesis with the pope who is pictured being carried on a palanquin. The motive of Christ carrying the cross was also taken up in the three Erfurt and two Strasbourg editions.

On 29 May 1521 the *Passional* had appeared in print in Wittenberg. On that day Bernhard von Hirschfeld, a councilman of the Elector Frederick the Wise, received a copy in Würzburg where he was staying on his journey back from the Diet of Worms. He sent this to the Nuremberg councilman Anton Tucher the Elder.[25] This date fits

---

[23] Benzing/Claus no. 1016, correspondingly in no. 1017 and in the Latin edition no. 1024.

[24] After swapping the subjects of the images the text underneath did not need to be changed, as both motives were contained in the original text, cf. edition below.

[25] Bernhard von Hirschfeld to Anton Tucher the Elder, Würzburg, 29 May 1521: *Euch thue ich neben dem ein neu gedruckts buchlein, welches ich alhie bekomen, Des inhalts habent ir zuvornemen; passional XRI [= Christi] auch ubersenden, in zuvorsicht, so fernne es gut grundig, ir werdet darab gut vormercken und auch gfallen entpfahen.* Ina Westphal, *Die Korrespondenz zwischen Kurfürst Friedrich dem Weisen von Sachsen und der Reichsstadt Nürnberg. Analyse und Edition* (Frankfurt am Main: Peter Lang, 2011), p. 552 (no. 377). This information was already included in Julius Köstlin, 'Briefe vom kursächsischen Hofe an A. Tucher in Nürnberg 1518-1523', *Theologische Studien und Kritiken* 55 (1882): 691-702 (p. 699). See also WA 9, 689-690.

with the fact that Luther on 26 May 1521 clearly had a printed copy of the *Passional* in his hands in the Wartburg.[26]

3. The Erfurt Editions of the *Passional*

The reprints of the *Passional* come from the workshop of the Erfurt printer Matthäus Maler († 1536)[27], the most famous Erfurt printer of the Reformation period.[28] Maler was repeatedly the first person to print texts from the circle of Wittenberg reformers, aided in part by Luther's Erfurt friend and confidant, the Augustinian prior Johannes Lang († 1548), acting as a go-between. In the first of his three editions of the *Passional*[29] Maler imitated every detail of the Wittenberg editions, including their typographical deficiencies.[30] Even the Wittenberg title page was taken over in the form of a recut into this print. Those interested in purchasing the pamphlet should have apparently had the impression that this was a Wittenberg print. The twenty-six woodcuts which illustrate the thirteen antitheses are very exact recuts[31], only ranking behind the woodcuts in the Wittenberg editions in terms of artistic quality. It is plausible that

---

[26] *Melanchthons Briefwechsel. Kritische und kommentierte Gesamtausgabe*, vol. T 1, ed. Richard Wetzel (Stuttgart-Bad Cannstatt: frommann-holzboog, 1991), p. 288, l. 22-23 (no. 141).

[27] Benzing/Claus no. 1020-1022; VD16 L 5579-5581. The sequence of the editions corresponds to the order of the three editions in Benzing/Claus. As with the Wittenberg editions, the Erfurt editions of the *Passional* do not name the printer, place of publication and publication date. The attribution to Matthäus Maler has a long tradition. In the copy of the Pitts Theology Library, Kessler Collection, Atlanta: 1521 Luth WW (Benzing/Claus no. 1022) a hand from the eighteenth or nineteenth century has noted on the title page: *gedr.[uckt] bey Matthä.[us] Maler in Erfurt*. WA 9, 694 also includes the same designation.

[28] Christoph Reske, *Die Buchdrucker des 16. und 17. Jahrhunderts im deutschen Sprachgebiet* (Wiesbaden: Harrassowitz, ²2015), p. 218.

[29] Benzing/Claus no. 1022.

[30] See Gustav Kawerau in WA 9, 693.

[31] See Koepplin/Falk 1974 (n. 3), vol. 1, p. 330, no. 218.

these recuts were produced in the workshop of Cranach in Wittenberg. In his second and third editions Maler moved away from the visual imitation of the Wittenberg editions by using his own title page, signed with the monogram *FB* of an unidentified artist, which shows an arched portal in the Renaissance style.[32]

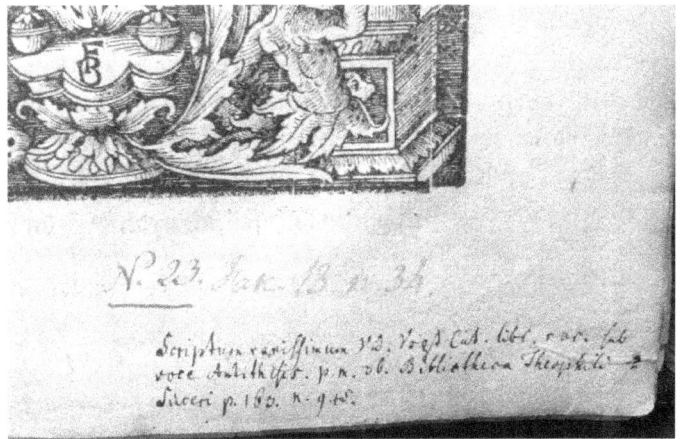

Both Oxford copies printed in Erfurt 1521 belong to the later editions with the monogram FB and the date 1521; for the Taylorian copy see below; here the copy Bodleian Library, Tr. Luth. 13 (34) where a later reader has added the appreciative statement that this is a most rare pamphlet (*Scriptum rarissimum*)

In a copy of Maler's third edition[33] a presumably contemporary hand has added the monogram *ICW* on every double page and always on the image of Christ.[34] If the letters *I* and *C* were abbreviations for the

---

[32] Reproduced in: Johannes Luther 1973 (n. 2), figs. 67 and 67a.

[33] Württembergische Landesbibliothek Stuttgart: Theol. qt. 5577-1 (Benzing/Claus no. 1022; VD16 L 5581).

[34] The monogram is always located in places where monograms of artists usually have their place, for example in the lower left corner. Additionally, this monogram is noted on the titlepage, next to the monogram *FB* which is included in the titlepage woodcut. Presumably the writer wanted to make it clear that only the title border was produced by *FB* and not the remaining woodcuts.

first and last names of this unknown person, then *W* could refer to
Wittenberg as the place of origin or activity of this person.

As a result of the new title page it is possible to determine the time
period in which Maler printed his *Passional* editions. The woodcut
which Maler used in his second edition[35] is marked by the year *1520*.
This is changed to *1521*[36] in the third edition.[37] Thus the woodcut
was produced in 1520 and Maler used it from this point onwards. A
printed text of Johannes Lang, presumably from June or July 1521,
still contains the title woodcut with the date *1520*.[38] The woodcut
with the updated year 1521 can also be found in the edition of the
German translation of Luther's *Judgement on Monastic Vows* (*Iudicium
de votis*).[39] The Wittenberg edition of the original Latin version of
this text was completed on 8 October 1521.[40] The translation went
to press soon afterwards under Maler. From this it is evident that the
Passional editions of Maler with the new title page went to press at

---

[35] *Passional Christi | vnnd Antichristi.* [Erfurt: Matthäus Maler 1521]. On the bottom
left of the title page border: *1520*. Landesbibliothek Coburg: Lu-59,616; the single
known copy, only containing the quires A and B. Benzing no. 1021; VD16 L 5580.

[36] *Passional Christi | vnnd Antichristi.* [Erfurt: Matthäus Maler 1521]. Benzing no.
1022; VD16 L 5581. In the title page border: *1521*. Pitts Theology Library, Atlanta,
Kessler Collection: 1521 Luth WW; Taylorian, Oxford: ARCH.8o.G.1521(19), see
the facsimile below of the titlepage; Bodleian Library, Oxford: Tr. Luth. 13 (34), see
above.

[37] Both versions of the title border are reproduced in: Johannes Luther 1973, fig. 67
and 67a. The change in the year has been carried out in the woodblock by cutting
out the right-hand half of the number 0 so that the remnants can be read as 1.

[38] Johannes Lang, *Joannis Langi ErPHVRDIENSIS Epistola ad Excellentiss. D. Martinum Margaritanum, Erphurdien.[sis] Gymnasij Rectorem pro literis sacris, & seipso.* [Er-
furt: Matthäus Maler 1521]. VD16 L 309. A letter of Lang contained in this print is
dated 4 June 1521. The prologue of Eobanus Hessus to the reader is dated *mense
Iunio.Anno. M. D. XXI.*

[39] Martin Luther: *Doctoris Mar. Lutther kurtz schluszrede von den gelobdten vnnd geystlichen leben der closter,* [Erfurt: Matthäus Maler 1521]. Benzing/Claus no. 980; VD16
L 5012, cf. WA 8, 320. The Erfurt print is the first edition of the translation.

[40] WA 8, 317.

some point between July 1521 and at the very latest the end of 1521. The updating of the year on the title page clearly happened during the typesetting of the *Passional* as the two *Passional* editions which use this title woodcut only differ in the printed year[41] while the type was not changed.

4. The Strasbourg Editions

In an expanded and considerably changed design, two further *Passional* editions appeared in Strasbourg which once again are silent about the names of the printers. The first edition was printed by Johann Prüss the Younger[42] and the second edition by Johann Knobloch the Elder[43], who took over the printed blocks of Prüss.

The sequence in which the editions were prepared can be reconstructed from a comparison of the quality of the woodcuts. There are signs of damage on the edges of some of the woodblocks in the printed copies of Knobloch's edition which cannot be seen in the printed copies of Prüss.

Broken border of the titlepage
in the second Strasbourg edition,
Bodleian, Tr. Luth. 250a

---

[41] This conclusion is limited solely to quires A and B as the single known copy of the edition Benzing/Claus no. 1021 only contains these quires.

[42] *Passional Christi vnd Antichristi. || Christus. | Petre/ wa[n] | würd enbun|den ich? |* […]. [Strasbourg: Johann Prüss d. J. 1521]. Benzing/Claus no. 1018 = VD16 L 5583. Universitätsbibl. Heidelberg: Q 3661-4. On Johann Prüss d. J. see Reske 2015, p. 955.

[43] *Passional Christi vnd Antichristi. || Christus | Petre/ | wa[n] würd | entbunde[n] ich?* [Strasbourg: Johann Knobloch d. Ä. 1521?]. Benzing/Claus no. 1019 = VD16 L5582. Bodleian Library Oxford: Tr. Luth. 250a. This edition repeatedly offers the better text. On Johann Knobloch d. Ä. see Reske 2015, pp. 952-953.

The first of the two editions can be dated to 1521 since the text, which is added to a newly conceived woodcut for the title page, notes that Pope Leo X (1513-1521), who died on 1 December 1521, was still in office.[44] The Strasbourg editions display a series of special features and additions[45]:

1. The thirteen antitheses of the Wittenberg original are taken over. Of the twenty-six woodcuts of the Wittenberg editions, twenty-five are used again but as a mirror image. In one image, the birth of Christ in the stable (VIII 15), the Wittenberg original is replaced by the woodcut of another artist who depicts the same motive and which was clearly available in the woodcut collection of one of the two printers. As this woodcut had a smaller format than the remaining woodcuts both printers filled the excess space by adding two borders. For this Prüss the Younger[46] and Knobloch the Elder used different decorative strips from their supplies.

2. After antithesis XII of the Wittenberg original (Christ driving the money traders from the temple / pope as trader in the temple) two additional antitheses were added which are marked in Table 2 as XII A and XII B, with the extra images numbered 27-30.

---

[44] The text to right of the title page woodcut: *Christus. Petre/ wan würd enbunden ich? Wie lanng verfolgt der Babst doch mich? Petrus. Jetz/ so Babst Leo mit seim gesind Mit offenn augen ist starblind.*

[45] On the particularities of the Strasbourg editions see WA 9, 693-95 and 713 and 715. Cf. Karin Groll, *Das „Passional Christi und Antichristi" von Lucas Cranach d. Ä.* (Frankfurt am Main: Peter Lang, 1990), pp. 98-101; Franz-Heinrich Beyer, *Eigenart und Wirkung des reformatorisch-polemischen Flugblatts im Zusammenhang der Publizistik der Reformationszeit* (Frankfurt am Main: Peter Lang, 1994), pp. 16-17.

[46] The vertical decorated border used by Prüss in his edition (see above) was also used several times in the following pamphlet: *History Von den fier ketzren Prediger ordens der obseruantz zů Bern jm Schweytzer land verbrant/* […]. [Strasbourg: Johann Prüss d. J. 1521]. VD16 M 7064.

Table 2: Additional Antitheses in the Strasbourg Passional

XIIA Rejecting or Collecting Money
  [27] = 19[47] Sending out of the disciples: Christ demands poverty of
  them: Matt 6:20; Rev 20:6
  [28] The pope sells indulgences.
XIIB Grazing or Devouring Sheep
  [29] Christ as the good shepherd: **John 10:4,11-13;** John 15:13
  [30] The pope as a ravenous wolf: [Matt 7:15][48]; Matt 23:4

The insertion of XII A after XII is motivated by the wish to criticise the indulgence trade more forcefully than in the Wittenberg original. In XII 25 there had previously been a depiction of the pope selling letters for money, which in the Wittenberg original the text interprets as the selling of *dispensations, indulgences, pallia, bishoprics, fiefs* and further privileges.[49] The Strasbourg compiler of the *Passional* bolstered the accusation that the pope was greedy through XII A. Here the pope stands before a sack bearing the inscription *a sack of indulgences for money*. In order to contrast this with Christ, the compiler did not create a new picture, but repeated the same available motive of the disciples being exhorted by Christ to commit themselves to poverty. In the second new antithesis, XII B, the theme of the pope's greed is continued with the insertion of two new images: while Christ the good shepherd cares for the wellbeing of his flock, the papal wolf has a man tortured by his henchmen, a group of clerics, until he vomits money. It is notable that in the texts accompanying these new antitheses only biblical quotations are used. There is therefore less emphasis placed on the opposition of Bible and canon law which was so important for the Wittenberg texts.

---

[47] Picture X 19 (sending out of the disciples) is repeated here.
[48] This Bible passage is quoted in the editions without reference to the source.
[49] *Passional* (edition by Prüss, Benzing/Claus no. 1018), fol. D1r.

3. The compiler added the medium of poetry to the images and prose texts by sharpening each antithesis with a German rhyming couplet and a corresponding Latin hexameter.[50] Over the new antithesis XII B, for example, we read: *Christ grazes his lambs truly. While the papal wolf gorges them cruelly* (*Christus sein scheflin / weit trewlich.* ☞ *So frißts der wolffs bapst grausamklich.*). The corresponding Latin hexameter, one part next to the image of Christ and the other next to the pope, reads: *Christ pastures the sheep, while he [the pope] rejoices in the blood of the poor* (*Pascuit oues Christus, / Inopis hic sanguine gaudet*). In every rhyming couplet the compiler places a manicule as a graphical N.B. mark before the second line referring to the pope. He therefore makes graphically clear that the intended aim of the publication is papal criticism, not a meditation on Christ.

4. The highpoint of the reworked and expanded version is a new title page[51], which appears in the form of a theatrical scene, as a sort of prelude to the *Passional*. In this scene the martyred Christ, accompanied by Peter, stands immediately before the pope, who is accompanied by a cardinal and two bishops. While Christ in his posture turns towards Peter, Peter and the pope gesture with their right hands as if they are speaking. The corresponding text in the borders, to the right of the image and below it, is formally composed like a script for a play:

Christ: O Peter, when might I be released?
How long is the pope going to persecute me for?

---

[50] All rhymes and hexameters are printed in WA 9, 692-693. Quoted here following the Strasbourg edition printed below.

[51] Reproduced in Groll 1990, p. 343, fig. 45 and in Thomas Kaufmann, *Die Mitte der Reformation. Eine Studie zu Buchdruck und Publizistik im deutschen Sprachgebiet, zu ihren Akteuren und deren Strategien, Inszenierungs- und Ausdrucksformen* (Tübingen: Mohr Siebeck, 2019), p. 659.

Peter: Now there is Pope Leo with his entourage.
With eyes open, he is purblind.

Pope: Stand naked, both wretched and without a roof
Wait until I reverse your poverty.
In power, honour, riches
Ostentatiously I conquer earth and the kingdom of heaven.

5. At the end of the edition (D4v, WA 9, 715, cf. edition below) an eight-line poem is appended, which states that the aim of the book is to clarify whether the pope is the Antichrist.

6. At the end a fictional colophon is added:

So that I may be snatched from the Great Flood
I have been printed[52] in Noah's ark.
   From the ark of Noah.

5. Reception of Hussite Traditions

The scenes depicted in the *Passional* are built on pre-existing traditions and set in motion a new process of transmission. Images and texts of both the Latin and German versions can be placed within this tradition. Correspondingly the question of historical reception can be taken in two directions. First: which traditions did the Wittenberg printers, the deviser of the programmatic picture cycle and the authors of the text draw upon? And secondly: how was the Wittenberg product received and continued by contemporary observers, readers and listeners? For the latter question we are still lacking sufficient research, not least as we need to assess a sample of the many still surviving printed copies, especially graphical and verbal remarks inserted by readers and viewers of the texts and images (*Exemplarforschung*). This section will initially address the first

---

[52] The Prüss edition (Benzing/Claus no. 2018) has *getruckt*. The Knobloch edition (Benzing/Claus no. 2019, see below D2v) has *geruckt*.

question concerning the models of the Wittenberg pamphlets, which is closely connected to questions about authorship.

Even contemporaries of the reformers were concerned with the question of the author of the anonymous *Passional*. In a glossed copy of the Wittenberg first edition[53] which survives in the Ratsschulbibliothek in Zwickau, an unidentified writer of the sixteenth century has noted on the title page: *Author John Huss* (*Author Iohannes Huß*).[54] For every antithesis the reader restates the quoted texts from the Bible and canon law in the margin.[55] He therefore underlines that he understood the core of the antitheses in the text to be the opposition of biblical statements with those of canon law. The writer was aware that antitheses about Christ and the pope had a firm place in the Hussite tradition and that illustrations of this existed, which could be compared to the model of the Wittenberg visual antitheses.[56] He concluded from this that the *Passional* had its origins in John Hus. It remains open whether the writer of the note in fact meant that Hus was the author of the *Passional*, or whether he only recognised Hus's thoughts in it.

As early as 1893 Gustav Kawerau, the editor of the *Passional* in the Weimar edition of Luther's works, brought together a series of sources, including visual representations, of the pre-history of the Wittenberg antitheses in John Wycliffe, Johannes Hus and the

---

[53] Benzing/Claus no. 1015.

[54] Ratsschulbibliothek Zwickau: 12.10.11 (8).

[55] A glossed page from the Zwickau copy (fol. C5r, Antithesis XII, 24) is reproduced in: Joachim Werner; Kristina Leistner, *Kostbarkeiten der Ratsschulbibliothek Zwickau* (Zwickau: 1979), p. 53.

[56] Inter alia through the opposition of biblical quotations and canon law. A comparison with the so-called *Jena Codex* is productive. On this see: *The Jena Codex. Facsimile* (Prague: Gallery, 2009) und *The Jena Codex. Commentary* (Prague: Gallery, 2009).

Hussite tradition.[57] Kawerau drew the conclusion: *It was not simply the original idea of the Passional but also a larger part of individual antitheses that were already available before Cranach in both word and image.*[58] This judgement of Kawerau is in my opinion correct if you replace *original idea of the Passional* with *original idea of the Antithesis figurata vitae Christi et Antichristi*. This is because the secondary use of the term *Passional* in the production process was a Wittenberg creation, as the latest research demonstrates.

6. Author of the *Antithesis* and *Passional*: Not Luther, but Philipp Melanchthon and Johannes Schwertfeger

The glosser of the *Passional* copy in the Realschulbibliothek in Zwickau regarded Johannes Hus as author of the *Passional* because he believed he recognised ideas of the reformer in the pamphlet. Gustav Kawerau justified the inclusion of the *Passional* in the Weimar edition of Luther's works with a similar method of argumentation: the texts of the *Passional* contained, according to Kawerau, the *spiritual property (geistiges Eigentum)* of Luther[59], with numerous parallels between the texts of the *Passional* and Luther's own writings which had appeared before it.[60] Kawerau did, however,

---

[57] WA 9, 677-685. Kawerau's compilation can be expanded by further Hussite sources. Groll 1990, pp. 21-28 has compared a selection of sources chosen by Kawerau with the *Passional*.

[58] WA 9, 684: *Nicht allein die Grundidee des Passionals, sondern auch schon ein großer Theil der einzelnen Antithesen desselben ist somit in Wort und theilweise auch im Bild vor Cranach vorhanden gewesen.*

[59] WA 9, 690.

[60] WA 9, 685-687. Kawerau emphasises Luther's text Warum des Papstes und seiner Jünger Bücher von D. Martin Luther verbrannt sind from December 1520 (WA 7, 152-186), which according to Kawerau seems to have been the template for Cranach's work (WA 9, 686). Kaufmann 2019, pp. 656-657, n. 894 notes above all the dependence of the Passional on Luther's *An den christlichen Adel deutscher Nation* (WA 6, 404-469) and counts up the antitheses which are already present in the 1520 treatise.

bring forward some arguments which actually speak against Luther as the author of the texts.[61] He presumes that Luther was only involved in an advisory capacity during the planning stage of the writing.[62] The fact that the *Passional* was accepted into the recognised standard edition of Luther's writings has – against the intention of Kawerau – led to Kawerau's opinions on the authorship question only in part being received into the relevant Reformation literature.[63] The *Passional* continues to be treated as a text authored by Luther in frequently-cited Luther bibliographies[64], handbooks[65] and library catalogues. One of the Oxford copies shows an 18th century reader eagerly coming to the same conclusion, that *the author of this book is Martin Luther*.

Hujus Libri Author est Mart: Lutherus ut videre est in Bibliotheca Cyprianica pag. 125.

---

[61] WA 9, 687-688.

[62] WA 9, 690. Kaufmann 2019, pp. 656-657 has similar considerations.

[63] From the recent literature see for example Lyndal Roper, *Martin Luther. Renegade and Prophet* (London: Bodley Head, 2016), pp. 209-210 (Philipp Melanchthon as compiler of the texts, Johannes Schwertfeger as contributor to the references from canon law); Kaufmann 2019, pp. 656-657. Sometimes both Luther and Melanchthon or Melanchthon alone are named as the compilers.

[64] In addition to Benzing/Claus cf. Kurt Aland, *Hilfsbuch zum Lutherstudium* (Bielefeld: Luther-Verlag, ⁴1996), p. 137, no. 555 under the heading *Passional*, while the *Antithesis* is not considered.

[65] For example, Ute Gause, 'Passional Christi und Antichristi', in: Volker Leppin, Gury Scheider-Ludorff (eds), *Das Luther-Lexikon* (Regensburg: Bückle & Böhm, 2014), pp. 534-535.

Marginal entry in Strasbourg 1521: Bodleian Library, Tr. Luth. 250a, A1v, referencing the Lutheran theologian Ernst Salomon Cyprian (1673-1745).

Luther at no stage laid claim to the authorship of the *Antithesis* or the *Passional*. In the first printed catalogue of the published writings of Luther[66] which appeared in 1528 in Wittenberg, neither the *Antithesis* nor the *Passional* are included. Not a single contemporary is known to have ascribed the pamphlet to Luther. The Wittenberg reformer made two comments about the *Antithesis* and *Passional* which shed light on the authorship question and which emerged at the time when the texts were written. The first comment was written by Luther in a letter to Spalatin on 7 March 1521 in the following context:

> Has Effigies Iussit Lucas a me subscribi et ad te mitti. tu eas curabis. Iam paratur Antithesis figurata Christi et pap(a)e, bonus pro laicis liber.[67]

> (These pictures should according to Lucas's instructions be signed by me and sent to you. You will take care of them. At the moment an illustrated Antithesis of Christ and the pope is being prepared, a good book for the laity.)

The extract contains two themes: first, it is about pictures which Luther should sign[68] and secondly about the *Antithesis* which is in preparation.

The first theme: Luther has received several images (*Has effigies*) from Cranach, which he should sign and send to Spalatin. In this letter

---

[66] *Verzeychung vnd Register/ aller Bu(e)cher vn[d] schrifften/ D. Mart. Luth. durch yhn ausgelassen Vom Jar M.D. xviij. Bis yns acht vnd zwenzigst.* Wittenberg: Georg Rhau, [1528] (Benzing/Claus No. 3070; VD16 L 3447). WA 38, 132-134. The text is also not included in the second edition of 1533, which includes a prologue by Luther (Benzing/Claus no. 3072).

[67] WA.B 2, 283, 23-25 (no. 385).

[68] With *tu eas curabis* the first theme is concluded. With *iam paratur* the second theme begins.

Luther was passing on the pictures to Spalatin, who should take care of them (*eas*). Some scholars identify the named images with the Antithesis woodcuts of Cranach.[69] But the word *effigies* is a term for an image reproduced according to an original, specifically a portrait[70] or sculpture. This term does not fit with the freely-formed scenes of Christ and the pope. In the last sentence of the note to Spalatin Luther actually links these more precisely – through use of the participle *figurata* – with the term *figurae*, i.e. visual-symbolic representations of the antitheses. The previously named *effigies* should be signed by Luther. I reconstruct the process as follows: Cranach sent several images of Luther and wanted Luther to sign these and to pass them on to Spalatin. Luther performed this task and sent the signed images on to Spalatin with the words *You will take care of them*.[71] Yet what was Spalatin supposed to do with the portraits signed by Luther? At the time Spalatin was in Worms with the retinue of Elector Frederick the Wise for the Diet. During the Diet

---

[69] Cf. Otto Clemen in WA.B 2, 284, n. 11.

[70] Cf. Anna Pawlak, 'Effigies Lutheri. Martin Luther im Bilderstreit der Konfessionen', in: Zaal Andronikashvili; Giorgi Maisuradze; Matthias Schwartz et al. (eds), *Kulturheros. Genealogien. Konstellationen. Praktiken* (Berlin: Kulturverlag Kadmos, 2017), pp. 411-443, esp. p. 420, fig. 4, where Cranach's copper plate *Luther with Doctoral Hat* (1521) is reproduced. The distich under the portrait reads: *LVCAE OPVS EFFGIES HAEC EST MORITVRA LVTHERI | AETERNAM MENTIS EXPRIMIT IPSE SVAE* (*This mortal picture of Luther is the work of Lucas. He himself expresses the eternal (picture) of his spirit*).

[71] Kaufmann 2021, p. 14 offers a different interpretation of Luther's letter to Spalatin of 7 March 1521: *Dem Schreiben war eine „[e]ffigies" beigefügt. Cranach habe ihn, so ließ Luther wissen, um eine Unterschrift für dieses Bild gebeten. Der Augustinereremit aber wollte diese nicht selbst liefern; stattdessen gab er die Aufgabe an Spalatin weiter.* Kaufmann contends that Cranach requested that he should write a printed inscription (*Inschrift*) to appear under the Luther portrait. Yet instead of Luther, Spalatin carried out this task. This interpretation by Kaufmann seems to have emerged from a misunderstanding. Cranach sent Luther not only one *effigies*, but several (*Has Effigies*). Spalatin should subsequently take care of these pictures (*eas*), not an inscription. That Luther refused to sign as requested by Cranach (*a me subscribi*) is not in the text. Rather Luther expresses the expectation that Spalatin will do what is necessary.

Luther portraits, depicted both with and without a nimbus, were being sold.[72] These were clearly treasured keepsakes. In view of the clientele who were present at the Diet, it could have been useful to send Spalatin portraits with an autograph so that Spalatin could donate them to selected people.[73] This was because the handwriting complemented the picture with an additional individual expression of the person portrayed.[74] Here we come across a publicity campaign undertaken by Spalatin, Cranach and Luther, with the stage made ready for the appearance of Luther in Worms organised by the electoral Saxon side.

The second theme which is addressed in the quotation from Luther to Spalatin provides evidence that an *Antithesis figurata* was in preparation. This piece of information connected Luther by association with the first theme because both themes had something to do with Cranach's current activities around Reformation propaganda. Luther formulated: the illustrated *Antithesis is being prepared (paratur)*. A linguistic parallel to this formulation in the

---

[72] Martin Brecht, *Martin Luther,* Bd. 1: *Sein Weg zur Reformation 1483-1521* (Stuttgart: Calwer Verlag, ²1983), p. 419; Thomas Kaufmann, *Erlöste und Verdammte. Eine Geschichte der Reformation* (Munich: C. H. Beck, 2016), p. 132.

[73] Four painted portraits from the Cranach workshop of Luther, Melanchthon, Johannes Bugenhagen and Justus Jonas were produced in 1543. One or two Bible quotations and their signature appear under each of the reformers in their own hands. These examples demonstrate what sort of value individual handwriting could have when attached to a portrait. (Reproductions of the portraits in: Ulrich Bubenheimer, 'Die Lutherbibel des Hallenser Schultheißen Wolfgang Wesemer. Ein Stück Kulturgeschichte von den Einzeichnungen der Wittenberger Reformatoren bis zur Ausstellung auf der Wartburg', in: *Schätze der Lutherbibliothek auf der Wartburg. Studien zu Drucken und Handschriften*, ed. Grit Jacobs (Regensburg: Schnell & Steiner, 2016), pp. 114-117.

[74] Cf. Ann Blair, 'Early Modern Attitudes toward the Delegation of Copying and Note-Taking', in: *Forgetting Machines: Knowledge Management Evolution in Early Modern Europe*, ed. Alberto Cevolini (Leiden: Brill, 2016), pp. 265-285. On p. 270 Blair quotes the statement of Erasmus (1528) that the handwriting of a man has the same individual quality as that of his voice.

passive which does not name a specific subject can be found in a letter of Luther to Johann Staupitz on 9 February 1521: *Hutten and many others are writing courageously in my favour and daily songs are being prepared which will delight this Babylon less and less (Huttenus et multi alii fortiter scribunt pro me, et parantur indies cantica, quae Babylonem istam parum delectabunt.*[75] Luther does not name here – analogously as with the *Antithesis* – the author or the authors of the satirical songs which are being composed on a daily basis.

Regarding Luther's involvement in the *Antithesis* and *Passional* his remarks simply reveal that he approved the publication and praised the writing. On 7 March 1521 he was aware of the plan and perhaps even that part of the *Antithesis* was being produced – a sign that he was in contact with the drivers of the project. Parallels in content between the *Passional* and the published writings of Luther cannot establish that he was the (co-)author.[76] Luther was surrounded by people who absorbed and understood his ideas and passed them on. Moreover, the pamphlet also contains references to the writings of other Wittenberg reformers, such as Andreas Bodenstein's 1520 pamphlet *On Papal Holiness (Von päpstlicher Heiligkeit).*[77]

A second statement by Luther about our text can be found in a letter to Philipp Melanchthon (1497-1560), written in the Wartburg on 26 May 1521:

> Passionale antitheton mire placet; Iohannem Schwertfeger in ea opera video tibi succenturiatum.[78]

---

[75] WA.B 2, 264, 31-32 (no. 376).

[76] Kaufmann 2021, pp. 16 and 18 also reaches this conclusion.

[77] Edition of Harald Bollbuck in: Thomas Kaufmann (ed.), *Kritische Gesamtausgabe der Schriften und Briefe Andreas Bodensteins von Karlstadt*, vol. 3 (Heidelberg: Verein für Reformationsgeschichte, 2020), pp. 413-485.

[78] *Melanchthons Briefwechsel. Kritische und kommentierte Gesamtausgabe*, vol. T 1, ed. Richard Wetzel (Stuttgart-Bad Cannstatt: frommann-holzboog, 1991), p. 288, l. 22-

(The antithetical Passional pleases me greatly. I see that Johann Schwertfeger was a co-helper to you in this work.)

Initially Luther praises here the *Passional*. Then he speaks of Johann Schwertfeger (c. 1488-1524) as a co-helper of Melanchthon. In my opinion we can therefore justifiably conclude that Melanchthon and the jurist Johann Schwertfeger, whose friendship with Melanchthon and Luther is evidenced from 1518[79], were involved in the composition of both the *Antithesis* and *Passional*. The assertion often quoted in the literature that Melanchthon authored the texts while Schwertfeger as a jurist contributed to the passages from canon law was originally an hypothesis which, is not, however, transmitted in the sources. Schwertfeger's position in the Wittenberg Reformation and why in particular he was involved in the composition of the *Antithesis* shall now be addressed in greater depth.

Johannes Schwertfeger had studied canon and civil law in Wittenberg from 1514 or 1515 and acquired the degree of Doctor of Law in the summer semester of 1521.[80] An unedited letter of Schwertfeger to Georg Spalatin of 22 November 1519[81] demonstrates how the young lawyer at the end of 1519 introduced the reformatory criticism of church abuses into the Faculty of Law.

---

23 (no. 141). Differently in WA.B 2, 347, 23-24 (no. 413) according to an erroneous transmission. My rendition and translation of this passage based on the edition in the WA.B must correspondingly be corrected: Ulrich Bubenheimer, 'Andreas Karlstadts und Martin Luthers frühe Reformationsdiplomatie. Thesenanschläge des Jahres 1517, Luthers 'Asterici' gegen Johannes Eck und Wittenberger antirömische Polemik während des Augsburger Reichstags 1518', *Blätter für pfälzische Kirchengeschichte und religiöse Volkskunde* 85 (2018): 265-302 (p. 300, n. 178).

[79] On Schwertfeger and his relationship to Melanchthon and Luther see Bubenheimer 2018, pp. 265-302 (pp. 299-300).

[80] *Ibid*. p. 299.

[81] Universitätsbibliothek Basel: G I 31, fol. 36. The letter is listed by Christine Weide, *Georg Spalatins Briefwechsel. Studien zu Überlieferung und Bestand (1505-1525)* (Leipzig: Evangelische Verlagsanstalt, 2014), p. 139, no. 303.

Schwertfeger informed Spalatin that he had theses distributed which he wanted to dispute on Sunday 27 November 1519. In a first part he would offer the arguments of truth (*veritas*), i.e. the Bible, in reply to the cunning of the *Officiales* (judges appointed by a bishop in a diocese). In further disputations he wanted to debate the right of so-called "First Requests" (*primariæ preces*) as well as the priestly absolution of murderers against which the bishops would wield their tyranny.[82] Schwertfeger presented himself here not simply as someone familiar with the legal practice of the *Officiales*, but also with the Bible[83] which he himself had studied. The *Officiales* were the representatives of the bishops in the exercise of episcopal jurisdiction. How closely both Luther and Schwertfeger stood together in their criticism of the activities of the *Officiales* is shown by further sources. In 1518 Luther had already denounced in his *Sermon on the Virtue of Excommunication (Sermo de virtute excommunicationis)* the secular practice of excommunication being practised by the *Officiales*.[84] After Schwertfeger had opposed the evil of the *Officiales* in his disputation theses in general terms, he criticised the episcopal *Officiales* in Meißen and Stolpen in particular in two letters written to Spalatin on 14 March 1520 and 1 June 1520.[85] In summer 1520, in his writing to the German nobility, Luther had demanded

---

[82] *Quo re comprobarem, quod uerbis tue dominacioni coram pollicitus sum emisi posiciones, Die Solis proxima disputaturus [...]. Mitto ad te mearum nugarum exemplar, iudica num dignae disputacione sint an secus. Metui non nihil ne in priore periodo in coelum me spuere plerique existimarent. Verumtamen quom Officialium maliciam probe meditatam haberem libitum est magis ueritatis (huic studuisse me arbitror) racionem habere quam Deliciis aurium magnatorum incrementum adiicere. Restant plura quae disputare constitui ut de primariis precibus. De homicidis a presbitero absoluendis in quibus episcopi Tirannidem exercent.* Universitätsbibliothek Basel: G I 31, fol. 36r.

[83] In keeping with the use of Wittenberg reformers *veritas* refers to the Bible. Schwertfeger often uses *veritas* in this sense.

[84] WA 1, 649, 9-19. On this see Thomas Kaufmann, *An den christlichen Adel deutscher Nation von des christlichen Standes Besserung* (Tübingen: Mohr Siebeck, 2014), p. 229.

[85] Universitätsbibliothek Basel: G I 31, fol. 45r und 47v. Schwertfeger himself came from Meißen and had contacts to its episcopal curia.

that the secular authorities limit the involvement of the *Officiales* in religious affairs.[86] Luther may well have known Schwertfeger's theses and it seems probable that they had both exchanged views on the problem.

Schwertfeger's role in the *Antithesis* therefore was not necessarily limited to providing sections from canon law to a set of antitheses which had already been developed by Melanchthon. Schwertfeger could also have himself conceived pertinent antitheses. How Melanchthon and Schwertfeger ultimately worked together remains uncertain at present. The further question of who could have prepared the translation of the Latin *Antithesis* into German has also not yet been investigated.

7. From the Burning of Papal Law to the *Passional of Christ* – Theological Aspects

On 10 December 1520, in front of the Elster Gate in Wittenberg, a highly publicised book burning took place. Luther threw a copy of the papal bull *Decet Romanum pontificem*, in which Pope Leo X had threatened Luther with excommunication unless he recanted, into the fire. In addition, books of canon law as well as the writings of Luther's opponents Johannes Eck (1486-1543) and Hieronymus Emser (1478-1527) also became victims of the flames.[87] Jens-Martin Kruse has convincingly shown a connection between the burning and the publication of the *Passional*:

> In a further act of communal bonding the Wittenberg reformers endeavoured to convey in visual form the geographically and temporally limited action of 10 December and its underlying insight

---

[86] Kaufmann 2014, pp. 228-229.

[87] Cf. the description of Jens-Martin Kruse, *Universitätstheologie und Kirchenreform. Die Anfänge der Reformation in Wittenberg 1516-1522* (Mainz: Philipp von Zabern, 2002), pp. 266-270.

into the opposition between Christ and Antichrist to a broader public. The result of these efforts was the Passional of Christ and Antichrist [...].[88]

Alongside the contrast of the behaviour of Christ with that of the pope the scenes with Christ, in their combination of text and image, contain a specifically Christological message: Christ is the model whom the Christian in shaping his life should imitate – including the pope as well. This can be illustrated by one example: three biblical quotations from the Gospels (John 4:6; Matt 16:24; John 19,17) support the image of Christ in VI 11. Under these references the key passage for following Christ in Matt 16:24 is quoted in its entirety in the Latin *Antithesis*: *Whoever wants to follow me must renounce himself and follow me. Matthew 16.* But in the Wittenberg first edition in German the corresponding woodcut is based not on Matt 16:24, but on John 4:6: *When Jesus has gone a long way, he became tired. John. 4.*[89] According to John 4:6, Jesus, wearied by his journey, sat down at Jacob's well in Samaria. The authors of the *Passional* brought Jesus' modesty and humility into this text: Jesus is shown in the image walking barefoot, with three disciples following (VI 11A), while the pope is carried on a palanquin (VI 12).

But within the framework of a work given the title *Passional* for the German edition, the motive of the ascetic Christ going by foot clearly was not considered sufficiently striking. Over the course of the printing of the different Wittenberg editions the motive was replaced[90] by the traditional Passion motive of Christ carrying his cross (VI 11B). Now the third biblical quotation in antithesis VI explains the image: *He himself carried the cross und went to the place*

---

[88] Kruse 2002, p. 271.

[89] WA 9, 706, 2. Antithesis, fol. B 2v: *Ihesus fatigatus ex itinere sedebat sic supra fontem. Iohannis. iiij.*

[90] From the third edition, Benzing/Claus no. 1016, in some of the copies. Afterwards also in the edition Benzing/Claus no. 1017.

that is called Calvary. 19.[91] The appeal of this quotation to follow Christ by taking up the cross therefore gains the concrete sense of a call to prepare oneself to suffer according to the example of Christ. The illustrated pope by contrast lives in luxury and forces *baptised Christians* to carry him on their shoulders.[92]

The concentration of the selection of images and texts from the life of Jesus, which allows his behaviour and claims to be contrasted with the pope, leads to the *Passional* containing not a single soteriological statement referring to Christ as saviour of sinful man. In the *Passional* the actions of Christ suffice as a model by which human action should orientate itself. This ethical dimension of Christology – Christ as *exemplum* – can also be found with Luther[93], even if it is not the primary concern of his Christology as he had developed it up to 1521. In his work *To the German Nobility of the Christian Nation (An den christlichen Adel deutscher Nation von des christlichen Standes Besserung)* (1520) Luther had already offered the antithesis between Christ going by foot and the pope being carried on the palanquin:

> Der selben grosz ergerlichen hoffart ist auch das ein heszlich stuck/ das der Bapst yhm nit lessit benugenn/ das er reytten odder farenn muge/ szondern/ ob er wol starck und gesund ist/ sich von menschen/ als ein abtgot mit unerhorter pracht/ tragen lessit. Lieber wie reymet sich doch solch Lucifersche hoffart/ mit Christo/ der zufussen gangen ist/ und alle seine Aposteln?[94]

> (Another example of the same scandalous pride is that the pope is not satisfied to ride or be driven, but, although he is strong and in good health, he has himself borne by men like an idol and with unheard-of

---

[91] WA 9, 706, 5-6.

[92] Cf. the Latin version, Antithesis figurata, fol. B3r: *Sic etiam fert crucem Papa, vt baptisati Christiani cogantur eum humeris suis portare.*

[93] Cf. Notger Slenczka, 'Christus', in *Luther Handbuch*, ed. Albrecht Beutel (Tübingen: Mohr Siebeck, [3]2017), p. 32.

[94] WA 6, 436, 10-14. Cf. Kaufmann, 2014, pp. 260-262.

splendour. Dear readers, how does such satanic pride compare with Christ, who went on foot, as did all his disciples?)[95]

If one compares Luther's antithesis of Christ who goes by foot and the pope who lets himself be carried with the corresponding antithesis in the *Passional* then it is clear that the antithesis in the *Passional* has been sharpened. While Luther only speaks of Christ going by foot, the *Passional* emphasises that Christ continued until exhausted. While Luther criticises the pope for letting himself be carried as an idol, then the *Passional* adds a further charge that the pope forces baptised Christians to carry him.

The reasoning behind the concentration of the *Passional* on the comparison of the life of Christ with that of the popes lay in the authors' intention to shock the readers' awe and veneration of the pope. The Christological model of Christ as *exemplum* is used as a theological frame of reference because it was popular in the piety of that time. Even Andreas Karlstadt (1486-1541) in his text *On Papal Holiness* (*Von päpstlicher Heiligkeit*) from Autumn 1520 contrasted the errors of Pope Leo X with the life of Christ.[96] In a piece of writing directed against Johannes Eck, Karlstadt had also in 1520 called upon Erasmus of Rotterdam († 1536), who had called Christ an *example* (*exemplum*) and *archetype* (*archetypus*) for the life of a Christian.[97] The *Paraclesis* of Erasmus quoted by Karlstadt[98] was probably familiar to both the Wittenberg humanists and an educated readership.

---

[95] LW 48, 168-169.

[96] Referenced by Kruse 2002, p. 265.

[97] Andreas Karlstadt: *VERBA DEI Quanto candore [et] q[uam] syncere praedicari,quantaq[ue] solicitudine vniuersi debeant addiscere.* [...],Wittenberg: Melchior Lotter d. J. 1520, fol. D3r. Edition of Harald Bollbuck in Thomas Kaufmann (ed.): *Kritische Gesamtausgabe der Schriften und Briefe Andreas Bodensteins von Karlstadt.* Vol. 3 (Heidelberg: Verein für Reformationsgeschichte 2020), p. 63, l. 13-23.

[98] Karlstadt quoted from Erasmus's *Paraclesis ad lectorem pium.* In the passage on Christ as exemplum Erasmus writes: *Siue quod discere cupimus, cur alius autor magis*

After the editions of the *Passional* and *Antithesis figurata* had come off the press in Wittenberg, an anonymous pamphlet appeared by the same printer, Johann Grunenberg, which was linked in image and text to the *Passional*: *A Lament and Plea of the German Nation to Almighty God for Salvation from the Prison of the Antichrist (Ein Klag und Bitt der deutschen Nation an den allmächtigen Gott um Erlösung aus dem Gefängnis des Antichrist).*[99] On the rear side of the title page one of the woodcuts from the *Passional* is printed, the image of the pope with his clergy, accompanied by mercenaries, riding to hell (IX 18 of the *Passional*).[100] The author of the *Lament and Plea* did not choose the last image of the *Passional*, the pope's descent into hell (XIII 26), but consciously the image in which not only the pope, but also his clergy, go into Hell. This is because the author of the *Lament and Plea* directs his criticism first towards the pope, and then towards the bishops, abbots, abbesses and mendicant monks, reaching the conclusion:

Alßo richt sich yderman nach dem Romischen Antichrist
   Bischoff/ Cardinal/ pfaff/ monich/ seyn hoffgesinde ist
Die sich alle mit dem Antichrist voreynet han
   das sie betrigen/ vnd vorfuren/ alle christen man.[101]

---

placet quam ipse Christus? Siue viuendi formam requirimus, cur aliud nobis prius est exemplum quam Archetypus ipse Christus? Desiderius Erasmus Roterodamus: *Opera omnia*, Tomus V, 7 (Leiden: Brill, 2013), p. 294, l. 201-203.

[99] *Eyn Clag vnd bitt der deutsche[n] Nation an den almechtigen gott vmb erloszu[n]g ausz dem gefencknis des Antichrist:* [Wittenberg: Johann Grunenberg], 1521 (Hans-Joachim Köhler, *Bibliographie der Flugschriften des 16. Jahrhunderts. Teil I: Das frühe 16. Jahrhundert (1501-1530)* (Tübingen: Bibliotheca Academica, 1991-1996) vol. 2, No. 2055). A linguistically simplified version which is not true to the original can be found in Oskar Schade (ed.): *Satiren und Pasquille aus der Reformationszeit*, vol. 1 (Hannover: Carl Rümpler, ²1863), pp. 1-6 and 179-180.

[100] The woodcut in the *Clag* shows greater damage in its borders than the one in the *Antithesis figurata*. From this we can conclude that the *Clag* was printed after the *Antithesis figurata*.

[101] *Eyn Clag*, fol. A4r; Schade 1863, p. 6, l. 171-174.

(Thus everyone conforms themselves to the Roman Antichrist
Bishop, cardinal, priest, monk, are his court retinue
They all have united with the Antichrist
So that they deceive and seduce all Christian people.)

The *Lament and Plea* carries over the opposition of the Bible and papal law from the *Passional*. However, in recourse to the Bible, the focus is not on scenes from the life of Christ. Instead of quoting from the Gospels, Saint Paul is placed at the centre:

> O Herre Jesu laß dich erbarmen
>   Das sie sich beweyssen ßo tyrannisch gen den armen
> Geschehe on nit me vnder deynen namen sulch geperde
>   Thu deyn gnade vnd straff sie hie auff erden
> Das sie widder kommen yn den rechten standt
>   Do tzu sie sanct Pauel vorbunden hat mit munde vnd hand.[102]

> (O Lord Jesus, take pity
> That they [the bishops] behave so tyrannically towards the poor.
> Such behaviour should no longer be done to them under your name.
> Show your mercy and punish them here on earth
> That they come once again into the right state
> In which St Paul has bound them with mouth and hand.)

Papal laws seduce people into wanting to demand salvation through works, rather than Christ alone, in faith, hope and love:

> O Ir Christen weynet vnd vorgisset blutige zern
>   das die heylige schrifft ist vndergedruckt mit gefern
> Den der Antichrist vnd großer anhangk
>   Die heylige geschriff han gestossen vnder dye bangk
> Ire gesetze/ vnd heydennisch kunst heruor getzogen
>   Do mit sye land vnd leuhte haben betrogen
> Das vil menschen durch yre werck selig hoffen zu werden
>   Szo doch/ alleyne durch Christum mussen hye auff erden

---

[102] *Eyn Clag*, fol. A3r; Schade 1863, p. 4, l. 101–106.

Mit heyligen glauben/ hoffnung/ vnd rechter liebe
  Szeligkeyt erlangen/ aber kommen zun hellischen dieben.[103]

(O you Christians cry and pour out bloody tears
Because God's Holy Word has been suppressed with deceptions.
As the Antichrist and his great retinue
Have placed the Holy Word under the bench
And pulled out their laws and heathen ways.
Through this they have deceived the land and its people
That many people hope to become saved through their works.
But yet it is only through Christ that they here on earth
Must seek their salvation with holy faith, hope and true love
Or else come to the hellish thieves.)

The *Lament and Plea* reads like a commentary on the *Passional*. The Christological model of the *Passional* is subtly expanded upon through the comments on salvation coming solely through faith. The orientation towards Luther's theology is unmistakeable.

Georg Spalatin passed on a copy of the *Lament and Plea* with a personalised dedication "To my gracious lord, Duke Johann Friedrich of Saxony etc. 1521" (*Meinem Gnedigen Hern Hertzog Hans Fridrich zu Sachssen etc. 1521*).[104] Johann Friedrich of Saxony (1503-1554, Electoral Prince 1532-1547) was a son of Duke Johannes of Saxony (1468-1532, Electoral Prince 1525-1532) and a nephew of the Electoral Prince Frederick the Wise. Spalatin had been Johann Friedrich's teacher and educator for a time at the court of Frederick the Wise. That Spalatin sent the *Lament and Plea* to the eighteen-year-old prince Johann Friedrich demonstrates how he was trying to make the future electoral prince familiar with the cause of the Wittenberg reformers and to promote their ideas.

---

[103] *Eyn Clag,* fol. A2r; Schade 1863, p. 2, l. 25-34.
[104] Note of Spalatin on the title page of the copy of the Pitts Theology Library, Emory University, Atlanta: 1520 CLAG A.

Bibliography

Abbreviations

Benzing/Claus   Josef Benzing, Helmut Claus: Lutherbibliographie, Baden-Baden, vol. 1, 1966; vol. 2, 1994.
c.   capitulum, canon
C.   Causa
Clem.   Clementinæ
CorpIC   Corpus Iuris Canonici, ed. Emil Friedberg, Leipzig ²1879–1881, 2 vols.
d.   Distinctio
Decr.   Decretum Gratiani
Decretal.   Decretales Gregorii IX
Extrav. com.   Extravagantes communes
Lib. Sextus   Liber Sextus Decretalium
LW   Martin Luther, *Luther's Works*, various translators (St Louis, 1957–86).
q.   Quæstio
VD16   Verzeichnis der im deutschen Sprachbereich erschienenen Drucke des 16. Jahrhunderts: https://www.bsb-muenchen.de/kompetenzzentren-und-landesweite-dienste/kompetenzzentren/vd-16/
WA   Martin Luther: Werke. Kritische Gesamtausgabe [Weimarer Ausgabe], Weimar 1883 ff.
WA.B   Martin Luther: Werke. Kritische Gesamtausgabe. Briefwechsel, Weimar 1930 ff.

Primary Sources

ANTITHESIS.‖ Das ist ‖ Kurtze beschrei=‖bung/ Christi vnd des ‖ Antichrists/ Darin jr beider ‖ Art/ lehr/ vnd thaten gegen‖einander werden ge=‖halten.‖ Jn deutscher sprach zu=‖luoren also nie außgangen (Heidelberg: 1563) [VD16 R 3101].

Antithesis de præclaris Christi et indignis Papæ facinoribus,: cum Dei decalogis mandatis Antichristi oppositis, cumq[ue] vtriusq[ue] morū descriptione: quemadmodum sancta Scriptura tradit. modio, sed vt in candelabro (Geneva: 1557).

Ein neus lied vom Antillchrist zu Rom vnd seinen ‖ Aposteln/ wie sie vns/ durch verschuldung ‖ vnser sunden vnd vndanckbarkeyt gegen ‖ got/ verfureth haben mit iren lehren ‖ gesetzen/ vnd gepoten/ dorin verllmant werden alle Christen ‖ solche verfurische lehr ‖ zu verlassen ‖ vnd die Euangelisch warheit ‖ anzunemen.‖ ... ‖ (Würzburg: 1523) [VD16 N 1237].

John Frith, A pistle to the Christen reader ‖ The Revelation of Antichrist.‖ Antithesis/ wherin are compallred to geder Christes actes ‖ and oure holye father ‖ the Popes.‖ (Antwerp: 1529) [VD16 ZV 26131].

History Von den fier ketzren Prediger ordens der obseruantz zu(o) Bern jm Schweytzer land verbrant/ [...]. (Strasbourg: Johann Prüss d. J. 1521) [VD16 M 7064].

Howard Kaminsky, Dean Loy Bilderback, Imre Boba and Patricia N. Rosenberg (eds), *Master Nicholas of Dresden The Old Color and the New. Selected Works Contrasting the Primitive Church and the Roman Church* (Philadelphia: The American Philosophical Society, 1965).

Thomas Kaufmann (ed.), *Kritische Gesamtausgabe der Schriften und Briefe Andreas Bodensteins von Karlstadt*, vols 2-3 (Heidelberg: Verein für Reformationsgeschichte, 2019-2020).

Heinrich von Kettenbach, Vergleychung ‖ des allerheyli=llgisten herren/‖ vnd vatter des Bapsts/ gegen ‖ dem seltzamen frembdē gast yñ ‖ der Christenheyt/ gnant Jesus/‖ der ynn kurtzer zeyt widderumb ‖ ynn Teutsch landt ist komen/‖ vnd yetzund widder will ynn ‖ Egypten landt/ als eyn ‖ verachter bey vns.‖ ... Bruder Heinrich kettenbach.‖ (Wittenberg: 1523) [VD16 K 836].

Julius Köstlin, 'Briefe vom kursächsischen Hofe an A. Tucher in Nürnberg 1518-1523', *Theologische Studien und Kritiken* 55 (1882): 691-702.

Johannes Lang, Joannis Langi ErPHVRDIENSIS Epistola ad Excellentiss. D. Martinum Margaritanum, Erphurdien.[sis] Gymnasij Rectorem pro literis sacris, & seipso. (Erfurt: Matthäus Maler 1521) [VD16 L 309].

Martin Luther, An den christlichen Adel deutscher Nation von des christlichen Standes Besserung (1520) (WA 6: 404-469).

Martin Luther, An den christlichen Adel deutscher Nation von des christlichen Standes Besserung, ed. Thomas Kaufmann (Tübingen: Mohr Siebeck, 2014).

Martin Luther, Warum des Papstes und seiner Jünger Bücher von D. Martin Luther verbrannt sind (1520) (WA 7: 152-186).

Martin Luther, Doctoris Mar. Lutther kurtz schluszrede von den gelobdten vnnd geystlichen leben der closter (Erfurt: Matthäus Maler 1521) [VD16 L 5012].

Christoph Marstaller, Der Welt vrlaub von den Menschen Kindern Vnd Wie der Jüngste Tag vor der Thůr / nach ausweisung der wort Christi / auch deren Zeichen / so Christus vor seiner andern Zukunfft vermeldet / Allen fromen Christen dieser letzten Zeit zur warnung / vnd ires Lebens besserung (Oberursel: 1563) [VD16 M 1137].

Melanchthons Briefwechsel. Kritische und kommentierte Gesamtausgabe, vol. T 1, ed. Richard Wetzel (Stuttgart-Bad Cannstatt: frommann-holzboog, 1991).

Simon Rosarius, Antithesis. Das ist Kurtze beschreibung / Christi vnd des Antichrists / Darin ir beider Art / lehr / vnd thaten gegen einander werden gehalten (Heidelberg: 1563).

Oskar Schade (ed.): *Satiren und Pasquille aus der Reformationszeit*, vol. 1 (Hannover: Carl Rümpler, ²1863)

Marta Vaculínová et al. (eds), Jenský kodex. Faksimilie [The Jena Codex. Facsimile] and Jenský kodex. Komentář [The Jena Codex. Commentary] (Prague: Gallery, 2009).

Lorenzo Valla, *Discourse on the Forgery of the Alleged Donation of Constantine. In Latin and English*, tr. Christopher B. Coleman (New Haven: Yale University Press, 1922).

Ina Westphal, Die Korrespondenz zwischen Kurfürst Friedrich dem Weisen von Sachsen und der Reichsstadt Nürnberg. Analyse und Edition (Frankfurt am Main: Peter Lang, 2011).

De Christo et Suo Adversario Antichristo. Ein Polemischer Tractat Johann Wiclif's aus den Handschriften der K. K. Hofbibliothek zu Wien und der Universitätsbibliothek zu Prag, ed. Rudolf Buddensieg (Gotha: Friedrich Andreas Perthes, 1880).

Secondary Sources

Kurt Aland, *Hilfsbuch zum Lutherstudium* (Bielefeld: Luther-Verlag, ⁴1996).

David Bagchi, 'Printing, Propaganda, and Public Opinion', in: *The Oxford Encyclopedia of Martin Luther*, ed. Derek R. Nelson and Paul R. Hinlicky, vol. 3 (Oxford: Oxford University Press, 2017), cols 187-209.

Franz-Heinrich Beyer, *Eigenart und Wirkung des reformatorisch-polemischen Flugblatts im Zusammenhang der Publizistik der Reformationszeit*

(Frankfurt am Main: Peter Lang, 1994).

Ann Blair, 'Early Modern Attitudes toward the Delegation of Copying and Note-Taking', in: *Forgetting Machines: Knowledge Management Evolution in Early Modern Europe*, ed. Alberto Cevolini (Leiden: Brill, 2016), pp. 265-285.

Curtis Bostick, *The Antichrist and the Lollards. Apocalypticism in Late Medieval and Reformation England* (Leiden: Brill, 1998).

Wolfgang Braunfels, Michael Nitz, 'Leben Jesu', in: *Lexikon der christlichen Ikonographie,* ed. Engelbert Kirschbaum, vol. 3 (Freiburg im Breisgau: Heder, 1971), cols 39-85.

Martin Brecht, *Martin Luther*, vol. 1: *Sein Weg zur Reformation 1483-1521* (Stuttgart: Calwer Verlag, ²1983).

James A. Brundage, *Medieval Canon Law* (London: Longman, 1995).

Ulrich Bubenheimer, 'Andreas Karlstadts und Martin Luthers frühe Reformationsdiplomatie. Thesenanschläge des Jahres 1517, Luthers 'Asterici' gegen Johannes Eck und Wittenberger antirömische Polemik während des Augsburger Reichstags 1518', *Blätter für pfälzische Kirchengeschichte und religiöse Volkskunde* 85 (2018): 265-302.

Ulrich Bubenheimer, 'Die Lutherbibel des Hallenser Schultheißen Wolfgang Wesemer. Ein Stück Kulturgeschichte von den Einzeichnungen der Wittenberger Reformatoren bis zur Ausstellung auf der Wartburg', in: *Schätze der Lutherbibliothek auf der Wartburg. Studien zu Drucken und Handschriften*, ed. Grit Jacobs (Regensburg: Schnell & Steiner, 2016), pp. 89-147.

Lawrence P. Buck, *The Roman Monster. An Icon of the Papal Antichrist in Reformation Polemics* (Kirksville, Missouri: Truman State University Press, 2014).

Lawrence P. Buck, '"Anatomia Antichrist": Form and Content of the Papal Antichrist', *The Sixteenth Century Journal* 42.2 (2011): 349-368.

Catherine Dejeumont and William Kemp, 'John Frith's *Antithesis of Christes Actes compared to the Popes* (1529) in relation to Heinrich von Kettenbach's *Vergleychung*', *Reformation* 12/1 (2007): 33-68.

Bobbi Dykema, Luther, Cranach, and the Passional Christi und Antichristi (Saarbrücken: OmniScriptum, 2017)

Peter Dykema and Heiko Oberman (eds), *Anticlericalism in Late Medieval and Early Modern Europe* (Leiden: Brill, 1993).

Mark U. Edwards, Jr., *Printing, Propaganda and Martin Luther* (Berkeley;

London: University of California Press, 1994).

Gerald Fleming, 'On the Origin of the Passional Christi und Antichristi and Lucas Cranach the Elder's Contribution to Reformation Polemics in the Iconography of the Passional', *Gutenberg-Jahrbuch* (1973): 351-368.

Johannes Fried, *Donation of Constantine and Constitutum Constantini. The Misinterpretation of a Fiction and its Original Meaning* (Berlin; New York: de Gruyter, 2007).

Ute Gause, 'Passional Christi und Antichristi', in: *Das Luther-Lexikon*, ed. Volker Leppin, Gury Scheider-Ludorff (Regensburg: Bückle & Böhm, 2014), pp. 534-535.

Karin Groll, *Das „Passional Christi und Antichristi" von Lucas Cranach d. Ä.* (Frankfurt am Main: Peter Lang, 1990).

Hans-Jürgen Goertz, *Antiklerikalismus und Reformation. Sozialgeschichtliche Untersuchungen* (Göttingen: Vandenhoeck & Ruprecht, 1995).

R. H. Helmholz, "Si quis suadente' (C.17 q.4 c.29): Theory and Practice', in: *Proceedings of the Seventh International Congress of Medieval Canon Law. Cambridge, 23-27 July 1984*, ed. Peter Linehan (Vatican City: Biblioteca Apostolica Vaticana, 1988), pp. 425-438.

Scott Hendrix, *Luther and the Papacy. Stages in a Reformation Conflict* (Philadelphia: Fortress Press, 1981).

Hans J. Hillerbrand, 'The Antichrist in the Early German Reformation: Reflections on Theology and Propaganda', in: *Germania Illustrata. Essays on Early Modern German presented to Gerald Strauss*, ed. Andrew C. Fix and Susan Karant-Nunn (Kirksville, Mo.: Sixteenth Century Journal Publishers, 1992), pp. 3-17.

Howard Jones, 'The German and Latin Versions', in: *Martin Luther, Von der Freiheit eines Christenmenschen / On the Freedom of a Christian*, ed. Howard Jones and Henrike Lähnemann (Oxford: Taylor Institution Library, 2020), pp. lxxii-xc.

Thomas Kaufmann, *Neues von „Junker Jörg". Lukas Cranachs frühreformatorische Druckgraphik. Beobachtungen, Anfragen, Thesen und Korrekturen*, s. l. et a. (Weimar: Herzogin Anna Amalia Bibliothek, 2021).

Thomas Kaufmann, *Die Mitte der Reformation. Eine Studie zu Buchdruck und Publizistik im deutschen Sprachgebiet, zu ihren Akteuren und deren Strategien, Inszenierungs- und Ausdrucksformen* (Tübingen: Mohr Siebeck 2019).

Thomas Kaufmann, 'The Reformations and the Media: Printing and the

Creation of Identity through Texts and Images / Buchdruck und Identitätsbildung: Die Ausbreitung von Protestantismus und Katholizismus als medialer Prozess. Der Buchdruck der Reformation und seine Weltwirkungen', *Archive for Reformation History* 18.1 (2017): 115-125.

Thomas Kaufmann, *Erlöste und Verdammte. Eine Geschichte der Reformation* (Munich: C. H. Beck, 2016).

Helmut Kind, *Die Lutherdrucke des 16. Jahrhunderts und die Lutherhandschriften der Niedersächsischen Staats- und Universitätsbibliothek Göttingen* (Göttingen: Vandenhoeck & Ruprecht, 1967).

Hans-Joachim Köhler, *Bibliographie der Flugschriften des 16. Jahrhunderts. Teil I: Das frühe 16. Jahrhundert (1501-1530)*, 3 vols (Tübingen: Bibliotheca Academica, 1991-1996).

Dieter Koepplin, Tilmann Falk, *Lukas Cranach. Gemälde, Zeichungen, Druckgraphik*, 2 vols (Basel; Stuttgart: Birkhäuser, 1976).

Jens-Martin Kruse, *Universitätstheologie und Kirchenreform. Die Anfänge der Reformation in Wittenberg 1516-1522* (Mainz: Philipp von Zabern, 2002).

Peter Kuschner, 'Images for the simple; words for the wise. Cranach's and Melanchthon's Passional', *Skript Historisch Tijdschrift* 21.4 (2014): 277-302.

Volker Leppin, *Antichrist and Jüngster Tag. Das Profil apokalyptischer Flugschriftenpublizistik im deutschen Luthertum 1548-1618* (Heidelberg: Gütersloher Verlagshaus, 1999).

Johannes Luther, *Die Titeleinfassungen der Reformationszeit.* Mit Verbesserungen und Ergänzungen von Josef Benzing, Helmut Claus und Martin von Hase (Hildesheim; New York: Georg Olms, 1973).

James Marrow, *'Circumdederunt me canes multi*: Christ's Tormentors in Northern European Art of the Late Middle Ages and Early Renaissance', *The Art Bulletin* 59.2 (1977): 167-181.

Bernard McGinn, *Antichrist. Two Thousand Years of the Human Fascination with Evil* (San Francisco: Harper Collins, 1994).

Rebecca Wagner Oettinger, *Music as Propaganda in the German Reformation* (Aldershot: Ashgate, 2001).

Anna Pawlak, 'Effigies Lutheri. Martin Luther im Bilderstreit der Konfessionen', in: *Kulturheros. Genealogien. Konstellationen. Praktiken*, ed. Zaal Andronikashvili; Giorgi Maisuradze; Matthias Schwartz et al.

(Berlin: Kulturverlag Kadmos, 2017), pp. 411-443.

Keith Pennington, 'Ecclesiastical Liberty on the Eve of the Reformation', *Bulletin of Medieval Canon Law* 33 (2016): 185-207.

Andrew Pettegree, *Reformation and the Culture of Persuasion* (Cambridge: Cambridge University Press, 2005).

Hans Preuß, *Die Vorstellungen vom Antichrist im späteren Mittelalter, bei Luther und in der konfessionellen Polemik. Ein Beitrag zur Theologie Luthers und zur Geschichte der christlichen Frömmigkeit* (Leipzig: 1906).

Christoph Reske, *Die Buchdrucker des 16. und 17. Jahrhunderts im deutschen Sprachgebiet* (Wiesbaden: Harrassowitz, ²2015).

Lyndal Roper and Jennifer Spinks, 'Karlstadt's *Wagen*: The First Visual Propaganda for the Reformation', *Art History* 40.2 (2017): 256-285.

Lyndal Roper, *Martin Luther. Renegade and Prophet* (London: Bodley Head, 2016).

R. W. Scribner, *For the Sake of Simple Folk. Popular Propaganda for the German Reformation* (Oxford: Oxford University Press, 1981, 1994).

Notger Slenczka, 'Christus', in: *Luther Handbuch*, ed. Albrecht Beutel (Tübingen: Mohr Siebeck, ³2017), pp. 428-439.

John Wei, *Gratian the Theologian* (Washington, DC: The Catholic University of America Press, 2016).

Christine Weide, *Georg Spalatins Briefwechsel. Studien zu Überlieferung und Bestand (1505-1525)* (Leipzig: Evangelische Verlagsanstalt, 2014).

Joachim Werner, Kristina Leistner, *Kostbarkeiten der Ratsschulbibliothek Zwickau* (Zwickau: Rat der Stadt Zwickau, 1979).

David M. Whitford, 'The Papal Antichrist: Martin Luther and the Underappreciated Influence of Lorenzo Valla', *Renaissance Quarterly* 61/1 (2008): 26-52.

Edition

1. Edition, Translation and Commentary
of the Latin *Antithesis of the Life of Christ and Antichrist in Pictures* and the German *Passional of Christ and Antichrist*

The first section contains an edition, translation and commentary of the Latin *Antithesis* (Wittenberg 1521, see the introduction by Edmund Wareham) and the Taylorian copy of the German *Passional* (Erfurt 1521). We provide a critical edition of the Latin text. We have silently normalised punctuation, as well as capitalisation, u/v, j/i, e/ae, qu/c (e.g. *cum* instead of *quum*) and m/n (e.g. *umquam* instead of *unquam*). We have replaced & with *et* and capitalised *Nomina Sacra*. *Jesus Christus* has been normalised. We provide the Bible citations as they appear in the original edition but then include a standardised reference in square brackets. We have maintained the word order of the original where it differs from the Vulgate. In the citations of canon law, we resolve any abbreviations and provide a full reference to Friedberg in square brackets. A critical apparatus is provided, which also indicates changes between the two Latin editions issued at Wittenberg (sigla A and B, see above chapter 2.2.; the Bodleian copy represents the A text). Because of the difficulties of citing canon law, in the English translation we retain the abbreviated forms c., q. etc. We mark the Incipits by italics (e.g. IX 18: Extravaganti *Super gentes*. John 22nd; VIII 16: 23 q. 5. c. *Omnium*) but only translate them if they make sense as a standalone unit (e.g. VII 14: c. *Inter cetera* on the office of the priests).

We then provide a diplomatic transcription of the Erfurt edition of the *Passional* held in the Taylor Institution. Given that a critical edition of the *Passional* already exists, we do not make changes to the text or provide an apparatus. The translation keeps close to the German version, maintaining specific features of it which cannot be found in the Latin. We have retained the references to the extracts from canon law in their original, abbreviated Latin form. While educated Latin readers with a legal background would of course have been familiar with the abbreviated citation system, we hope to render to readers how it might have seemed for German readers of the time with no legal training. In the cases where Latin words are retained in the main body of the German text (e.g. *animalia ventris*; *animals of the belly*) we have italicised the English translation to mark the language shift. For the translation of the Bible passages we have turned to Tyndale's versions of the New Testament (1526 and 1534) and the King James Version for inspiration, but not simply quoted it, given that the authors seem to have been quoting from memory.[1]

Following the edition and translation, we provide a brief description of the woodcut and a commentary on the two versions. This includes references to the Strasbourg edition and in the section that follows we provide a facsimile, edition and translation of the expanded edition held in the Bodleian Library. We offer a diplomatic transcription and translation of all the new elements, including the extra two sets of contrasts. We have not retranslated the main text blocks underneath each image for reasons of space. We refer to any significant differences in the commentaries.

---

[1] On this point see Catherine Dejeuomont and William Kemp, 'John Frith's *Antithesis of Christes Actes compared to the Popes (1529)* in relation to Heinrich von Kettenbach's *Vergleychung*', *Reformation* 12/1 (2007): 33-68 (p. 44, n. 28).

Titlepage (A1r)

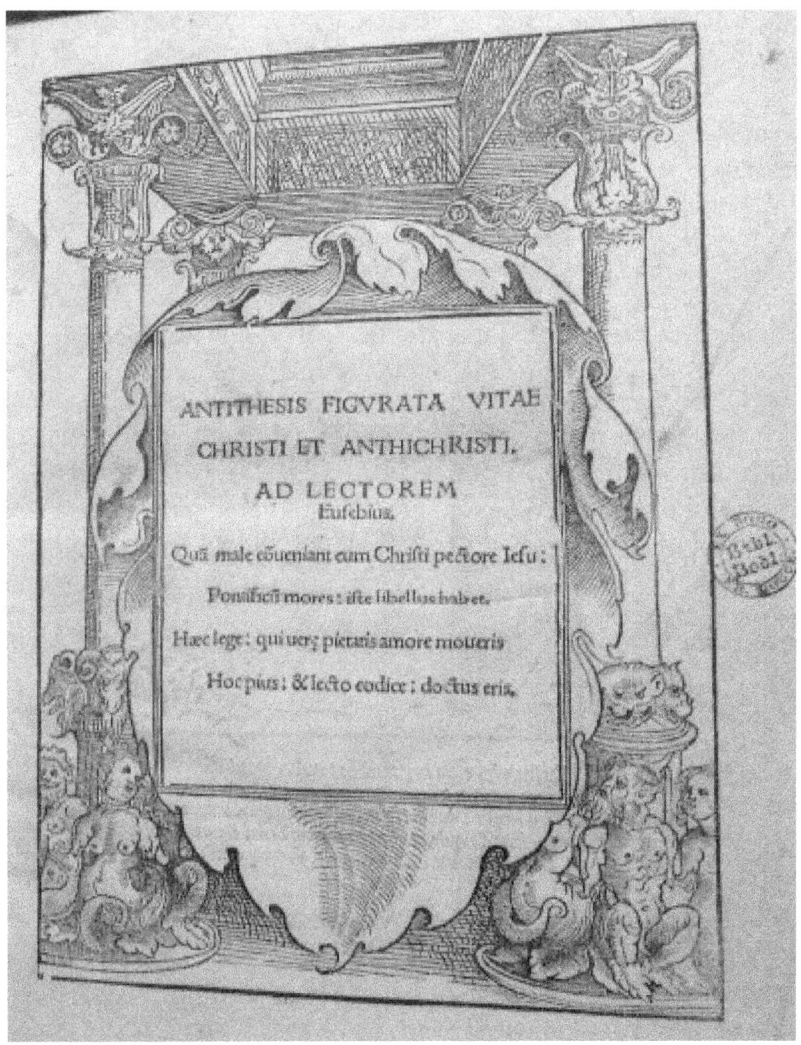

The ornamental border of the titlepage of the Bodleian copy of Wittenberg 1521,
cf. the introduction by Bubenheimer §2

Latin

ANTITHESIS
FIGURATA VITÆ CHRISTI ET ANTICHRISTI[2].

Ad lectorem Eusebius.
Quam male conveniant cum Christi pectore Jesu
Pontificum mores, iste libellus habet.
Haec lege, qui verae pietatis amore moveris.
Hoc pius, et lecto codice, doctus eris.

Antithesis of the Life of Christ and Antichrist in Pictures

Eusebius: To the reader.
How badly the customs of the pope conform with the spirit of Jesus
Christ can be shown by this little book. Read this whoever is driven
by love of true piety. When you have read this volume, you will be
pious and learned.

---

[2] ANTICHRISTI] *ANTHICHRISTI.*

German (Erfurt)

The ornamental border of the titlepage of the
Taylorian copy of Erfurt 1521 shows that this
is the third or later edition printed by
Matthäus Maler, cf. the introduction by
Bubenheimer §3

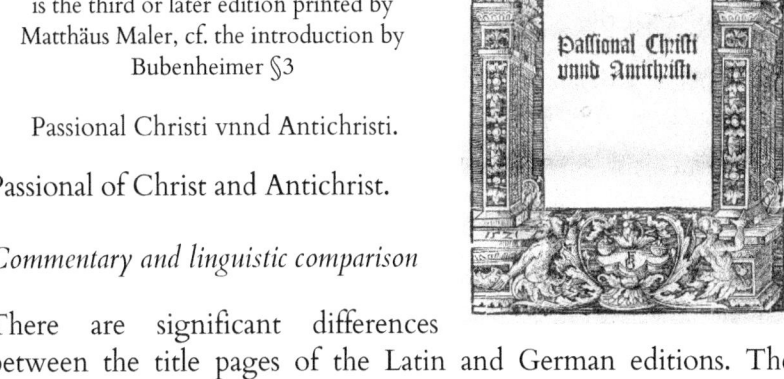

Passional Christi vnnd Antichristi.

Passional of Christ and Antichrist.

Commentary and linguistic comparison

There are significant differences
between the title pages of the Latin and German editions. The
German work is given the title *Passional*. A *Passional* was a small
illustrated book which contained scenes from the life of Christ or the
saints for the unlearned. The scenes from the life of Christ were
presented chronologically, with a particular emphasis on Christ's
Passion (the account of his final days). Cranach, Melanchthon and
Schwertfeger's *Passional* adapted this, by drawing on scenes
predominantly from Christ's entire life and not just his Passion. In
addition, they did not present the images chronologically, but rather
in such a way as to accentuate the contrasts with the life of the
Antichrist/pope.

The use of the word *figurata* in the Latin title indicates that this was
a book with pictures, but it chooses the more pointed term of
Antithesis, which foregrounds the intention of the work in a way that
is not present in the *Passional*. Indeed, from the title of the work
alone, one might have supposed that the *Passional* was a meditative
work, and this seems to have been a conscious decision on the part
of the Wittenberg reformers to camouflage the true intentions
behind the work [Kaufmann 2019:652].

Underneath the Latin title is a dedication from the figure Eusebius to an anonymous reader, and then four lines of verse. The verse draws attention to the fact that this is a *little book* that must be *read* and that it contrasts Christ and the pope in order to increase piety and learning. That the poem was not included in the German version is a further indication that the reformers sought to conceal the work's content.

The Strasbourg title page contains significant changes. It includes a scene of the martyred Christ, accompanied by Peter, standing before the pope, two bishops and a cardinal. To the right of the image and beneath it, a dialogue is printed, almost like a script of a play, between Christ, Peter and the pope. Criticism is directed specifically towards Pope Leo (1475-1521) and his entourage.

The Antichrist was based on several New Testament passages and refers to an antagonist of Christ who would make an appearance towards the end of time. Christian belief would be distorted into its very opposite until Christ would come and dethrone the Antichrist. Specific identifications of popes as Antichrist predated the Reformation, as did many of the contrasts which appeared in the *Passional/Antithesis figurata*. In the fourteenth century, the Oxford professor John Wycliffe had written a Latin polemic, *On Christ and his Adversary the Antichrist* (*De Christo et suo adversario Antichristo*) in which he provided twelve antitheses comparing Christ to the pope [*De Christo* 1880]. Such antithetical treatments also became an established part of Hussite anti-papal polemic of the fourteenth and fifteenth centuries. Master Nicholas of Dresden's 1412 *The Tables of the Old Colour and the New* (*Tabulæ veteris et novi coloris*), for example, contrasted the poverty and humility of Christ with the wealth and power of the pope [Kaminsky et al. 1965]. What changed with the onset of the Protestant Reformation was the identification of the entire papacy, and not just a single pope, as Antichrist.

I 1: Christ refuses the crown (A1v)

Christ, the bearded figure on the left, flees from the offer of a royal crown. The crowd offering the crown include men and women. Christ moves towards a forest, while a castle and city wall are visible in the top right hand corner.

Latin

> Christus: Jesus ergo cum cognovisset, quia venturi essent ut eum raperent[3], et facerent regem, fugit iterum in montem ipse solus. Iohan. vi. [John 6:15]. Regnum meum non est de hoc mundo. Iohan. xviii. [John 18:36]. Reges gentium dominantur eorum, et qui potestatem habent benefici vocantur. Vos autem non sic, sed qui major vestrum fuerit, sit tamquam minor. Luce. 22. [Luke 22:25-26].

Christ: When Jesus therefore had realised that they were about to come to seize him and make him king, he escaped again to the mountain, he alone (John 6). My kingdom is not of this world (John 18). The kings of the Gentiles rule over them and those who hold power are called beneficent. Yet you shall not be so, but he who is the greater among you let him be as the lesser (Luke 22).

German (Erfurt)

> Christus. Do Jhesus innen wardt / das sie kommen wurden vnd yhnen tzum kŏnig machen / ist er abermals vffin bergk geflohen / er allein. *Johan. 6.* Mein reich ist nicht von diszer welt. *Joh. 18.* Die kŏnige der welt hirschen yr / vnnd die gewaldt haben / werden gnedige hern genandt / yr aber nicht alszo / sonder der do grosser ist vnther euch / sall sich nydern / als der weniger. *Luce. 22.*

---

[3] raperent] B, *raperetur* A.

Christ: When Jesus became aware that they were going to come and make him king, he escaped again to a mountain, he alone (John 6). My kingdom is not of this world (John 18). The kings of the world rule over them and those who hold power are called gracious lords. Yet you shall not be so, but he who is greater among you shall humble himself as the lesser (Luke 22).

Commentary and linguistic comparison

The three biblical passages which are cited all relate to the theme of kingship. The image refers to the first biblical passage, John 6:15. Having seen Jesus perform the miracle of feeding the five thousand, the people believe him to be the Prophet. Jesus flees from them before they are able to make him king by force. In John 18, Pilate questions Jesus why it is that the Jews and chief priests have handed him over and what it is that he has done, to which Jesus responds that "My kingdom is not of this world". Luke 22 recounts the Last Supper. After Jesus has broken the bread and taken the cup, a dispute arose among the disciples as to which of them was considered to be greatest. Jesus responds with the passage which is cited.

The three passages can all be found in Lorenzo Valla's *Discourse on the Forgery of the Alleged Donation of Constantine* [Valla 1922: 54-55]. The Donation of Constantine claimed to reproduce the gifts of the Western Empire, the lands of Italy and the primacy over other patriarchal sees which Emperor Constantine the Great granted Sylvester, Bishop of Rome, in 314/315. The *Constitutum Constantini*, the forged text of Constantine's constitution, was written after the middle of the eighth century and came to be inserted into the twelfth-century collection of canon law, the *Decretum Gratiani*. In 1440 the Italian humanist, Lorenzo Valla (1407-1457), exposed this as a forgery, in a text which was printed by Ulrich von Hutten in 1520 [Fried 2007; Whitford 2008]. Valla uses these passages to emphasise that Christ had nothing to do with secular sovereignty and that when he was offered a kingdom of this sort, he would not accept it.

While the quotations from the Vulgate are for the most part precise in the text as a whole, in these quotations there are some differences. *eum* is omitted between *facerent regem* and *super eos* between *habent benefici*. The B edition corrects the incorrect third person singular imperfect passive subjunctive form of *rapio* (*raperetur*) with the correct active form (*raperent*). *[S]ed qui major est in vobis, fiat sicut minor* from the Vulgate is rendered differently as *sed qui major vestrum fuerit, sit tamquam minor*.

The German in this passage indicates that it has been translated from the Latin, rather than vice versa, in particular the position of *er allein* (*ipse solus*) at the end of the sentence [Kaufmann 2019: 650, n. 872]. The *er* is removed in the Strasbourg edition. Both German translations omit the phrase that they were going to seize him by force (*ut eum raperent*). The inclusion of the verb *sich nydern* (NHG: sich erniedrigen) emphasises the importance of Christ's humility, a virtue which is emphasised frequently in the subsequent images.

Erfurt edition:
Do Jhesus innen wardt / das sie kommen wurden vnd yhnen tzum kōnig machen / ist er abermals vffin bergk geflohen / er allein.

Strasbourg edition:
§ Do Jesus jnnen ward / das sie kummen würden / vnd yn zů einem künig machē / ist er abermals vff einē berg geflohē / allein.

I 2: The pope accepts the crown (A2r)

The pope, wearing the triple crown (tiara), stands with other representatives of the clergy (bishops / abbots; cardinals) before a group of armed mercenaries and two cannons behind a chain. The papal coat of arms, a pair of crossed keys, appears above them at the top of the archway. A group of knights in armour ride to meet them.

Latin

> Antichristus: Nos tam[4] ex superioritate, quam ad imperium[5] non est dubium nos habere, quod ex potestate, in quam vacante[6] imperio imperatori succedimus. Cle. pastoralis ad finem de sen. et re iudi. [Clem., II 11 c. 2, CorpIC 2, 1153]. Summa summarum: Aliud nihil est in iure canonico Papæ invenire: nisi ut suum idolum et antichristum super omnes cæsares[7], reges et principes extollat, sicut S. Petrus prius prædexit: Venturos pseudoprophetas dominationem contemnentes. [2 Petri 2: 1, 10].

Antichrist: We as well as by the sovereignty which we without doubt have to the Empire, as also by the power whereby we succeed the Emperor in the vacancy of Empire (Cle. *pastoralis,* towards the end on the pronouncement and judgement). In summary: Nothing else can be found in the pope's canon law than that he raises his idol and antichrist above all emperors, kings, and princes, as Saint Peter previously foretold: There will come pseudo-prophets despising domination.

---

[4] tam] *eam.*
[5] ad imperium] *ab imperio.*
[6] vacante] B, *vocante* A.
[7] cæsares] B, *cesares* A.

German (Erfurt)

Antichristus. Auß obirkayt die wir sonder tzweiffell tzum keyszer-
thumb haben / vnd ausz vnser gewalt / seynt wir des keysertumbs / so
sich das vorledigt / ein rechter erbe. *cle. pastoralis ad fi. de sen. et re. iudi.
Summa summarum.* Nichts anders ist in des Bapsts geystlichen rechte tzu
finden / dan das es seynen abgot vnd Antichrist vbir alle keyszer / kŏnig
vnd fursten yrhebet / als Petrus vorgesagt hat. Es werden kommen
vnuorschambte Bischoff die die weltlich herschafft werden vorachten.
2. Pet. 2.

Antichrist: Because of the authority which without doubt we have
over the Empire and because of our power, we are the true heirs of
the Empire, if it falls vacant (Cle. *pastoralis,* towards the end on the
pronouncement and judgement). In summary: Nothing else can be
found in the pope's canon law than that he raises his idol and
antichrist above all emperors, kings, and princes, as Peter foretold:
There will come unashamed bishops who will despise worldly
dominion (2 Peter 2).

Commentary and linguistic comparison

The first quotation was taken from the *Pastoralis,* issued in 1313 by
Pope Clement V, which decreed that the kingdom of Sicily lay
outside the jurisdiction of the Empire and emphasised the primacy of
the papacy over the Empire. This attracted the ire of Martin Luther
in his 1520 treatise *To the Christian Nobility of the German Nation
Concerning the Reformation of the Christian Estate*: "It is also ridiculous
and childish for the pope, on the basis of such perverted and deluded
reasoning, to claim in his decretal *Pastoralis* that he is rightful heir to
the empire in the event of a vacancy. Who has given him this right?
Was it Christ when he said, "The princes of the Gentiles are lords,
but it shall not be so among you"? Or did Peter bequeath it to him?
It makes me angry that we have to read and learn such shameless,
gross, and idiotic lies in the canon law, and must even hold them as
Christian doctrine when they are devilish lies" [LW 44.1:165-166].

Without reference to canon law, Luther also criticises this in his 1520 treatise, *Why the Books of the Pope and His Disciples Were Burned*: "He holds to be true and fosters the great unchristian lie that Emperor Constantine has given him Rome, land, empire, and power on earth [...] He boasts he is the heir of the Roman empire, although everyone well knows that the spiritual and secular realms do not get along well with each other" [LW 31.1:390].

The second half of the text also seems to have its roots in Luther's *Nobility*: "This most extreme, arrogant, and wanton presumption of the pope has been devised by the devil, who under cover of this intends to usher in the Antichrist and raise the pope above God, as many are now doing and even have already done. It is not proper for the pope to exalt himself above the temporal authorities, except in spiritual offices such as preaching and giving absolution. In other matters the pope is subject to the crown, as Paul and Peter teach in Romans 13:1–7 and I Peter 2:13, and as I have explained above. The pope is not a vicar of Christ in heaven, but only of Christ as he walked the earth. Christ in heaven, in the form of a ruler, needs no vicar, but sits on his throne and sees everything, does everything, knows everything, and has all power. But Christ needs a vicar in the form of a servant, the form in which he went about on earth, working, preaching, suffering, and dying. Now the Romanists turn all that upside down. They take the heavenly and kingly form from Christ and give it to the pope, and leave the form of a servant to perish completely. He might almost be the Counter-Christ, whom the Scriptures call Antichrist, for all his nature, work, and pretensions run counter to Christ and only blot out Christ's nature and destroy his work" [LW 44.1:165].

The Latin edition A contains two typographical errors (*eam* instead of *tam* and *vocante* instead of *vacante*), the latter of which is corrected in B. It also diverges from the original wording of the decretal through the inclusion of *ab imperio* (from the Empire) instead of *ad imperium* (to the Empire). Given that the German translation renders this as *zum keyßerthumb* (to the Empire), this would seem to be a mistake.

The quotation ascribed to the Second Epistle of Peter in the Latin combines two verses. The German translation heightens the anti-clerical element by rendering pseudo-prophets (*pseudoprophetas*) as unashamed bishops (*vnuorschambte Bischoff*). Words such as *gewalt*, *kŏnig* and *herschafft* mirror the vocabulary of the opposing page, further heightening the contrast between Christ, who rejects secular rule, and the pope, who embraces it.

The papal court in the Erfurt edition (left) and the Strasbourg edition (right) where a third cannon is added and the coat of arms is made more prominent.

II 3: Christ is crowned with thorns (A2v)

Christ, clothed in a robe, is mocked and tortured, with men pressing the crown of thorns onto his head with long sticks. The dog in the foreground points to Christ's tormentors being like dogs and builds on a reference to Ps 21,17 [Marrow 1977; Dykema 2017:42].

Latin

> Christus: Milites plectentes coronam de spinis, imposuerunt capiti eius, et veste purpurea circumdederunt[8] eum. Iohan: XIX. [John 19:2].

Christ: The soldiers plaited a crown of thorns, pressed it on his head and clothed him in a purple robe (John 19).

German (Erfurt)

> Christus: Die soldner haben geflochten eyne kronen von dŏrnen / vnd auff sein heubt gedruckt / darnach mit eynem purper kleydt haben sie yn bekleydet *Johan. 19.*

Christ: The soldiers plaited a crown of thorns and pressed it on his head, then clothed him in a purple robe (John 19).

Commentary and linguistic comparison

The second pair of images builds on the first pair through its focus on rulership. The quotation is taken from the Passion narrative in the Gospel of John, in which Jesus is sentenced to be crucified.

---

[8] circumdederunt] *circundederunt.*

II 4: The pope is crowned with a tiara (A3r)

Two bishops crown the pope, who sits on a dais, wearing a tiara and a cloak. A bishop with a crosier and thurible and two tonsured monks are below. A group of clerics stand in the background, while through a doorway a battle takes place.

Latin

> Antichristus: Imperator Constantinus tradidit nobis coronam imperialem, phrygium, chlamydem purpuream, tunicam coccineam et imperialia indumenta et sceptra. c. Constantinus xcvi. dist. [Decr., d. 96 c. 13-14, CorpIC 1, 342]. Eiusmodi mendacia ad tuendam tyrannidem suam confinxerunt contra omnes et historias et annales. Necquam enim umquam in more fuit Romanis imperatoribus tales gestare coronas.

Antichrist: The Emperor Constantine has given us the imperial crown, tiara, purple mantle, scarlet tunic and all the imperial raiment and sceptres (c. *Constantinus* dist. 96). They have fabricated lies of this sort to preserve their tyranny against both all histories and annals. For it was never customary for the Roman Emperors to wear such crowns.

German (Erfurt)

> Antichristus: Der Keyser Constantinus hat vns die keyserlich krone / getzirde allen andern geschmuck in massen wie yhn der keyser tregt / purper cleyt alle andere cleyder vnd scepter zutragen vnd tzubrauchen geben. c. *Constantinus. cxvi. dis.* Solche lůgen haben sie yre tyranney tzu erhalten erticht wyder alle historien vnd kuntschafft dan es ist nit brauchlich geweßen den Romischen Keysern ein solche krone tzutragen.

Antichrist: The Emperor Constantine has given us to wear and to use the imperial crown, ornaments and all other regalia just as the emperor wears them, the purple robe, all other robes and the sceptre (c. *Constantinus* dist. 96). They have composed such lies to uphold their tyranny against all histories and accounts. For it has not been customary for the Roman Emperors to wear such a crown.

Commentary and linguistic comparison

The first part of the text is not a direct quotation from the *Constitutum Constantini*, the forged text of Constantine's constitution, but rather bundles a number of different elements from its sixteenth chapter [Kaufmann 2019:665-667, n. 925], which was later taken up in the *Decretum Gratiani*: "We also therefore decree this, that he himself and his successors might use and bear upon their heads – to the praise of God for the honour of the Blessed Peter – the diadem, that is, the crown which we have granted him from our own head, of purest gold and precious gems" [Valla 1922:15-16]. The verbs *uti* (to use) and *gestare* (*to wear*) are not used in this sentence of the *Antithesis*, but are adopted in the *Passional* (*zutragen vnd tzubrauchen*). The German uses the singular form of crown in the final sentence whereas the Latin adopts the plural.

The word *phrygium* refers to the original form of the papal tiara, a kind of white Phrygian cap [Schramm 1935]. The second part of the text is a biting authorial commentary, in which one of the central defences of the Catholic side, namely custom and tradition, is undermined. It is clear that Schwertfeger and/or Melanchthon had read chronicles or annals on this issue. It remains unclear, however, which sources both authors could have used.

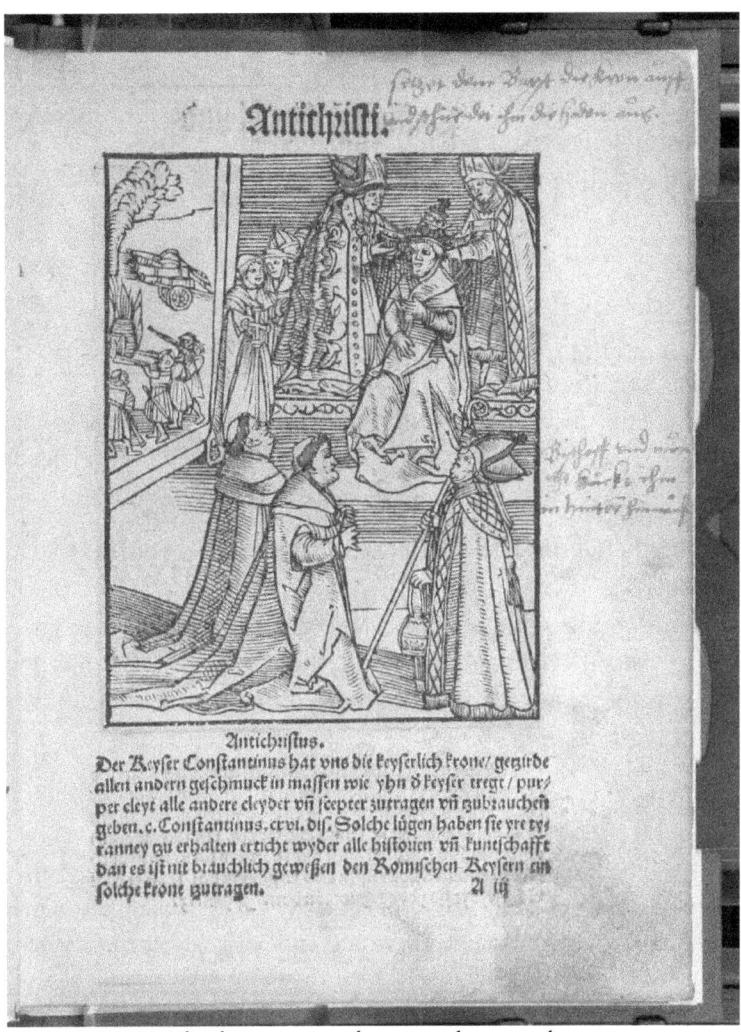

III 5: Christ washes the disciples' feet (A3v)

Christ washes and kisses the feet of one of the disciples, while the others watch on.

Latin

> Christus: Si ego lavi pedes vestros, Dominus et Magister, et vos debetis alter alterius lavare pedes. Exemplum enim dedi vobis, ut quemadmodum ego feci vobis, ita et vos faciatis. Amen, amen dico vobis, non est servus major domino suo, neque apostolus major est eo qui misit illum. Si hæc scitis, beati eritis si feceritis ea. [John 13:14-17].

Christ: If I then, your lord and master, have washed your feet, so even more should you wash one another's feet. For I have given you an example, that you should do as I have done to you. Verily, verily, I say unto you: The servant is not greater than his lord; neither an apostle greater than he that sent him. If you know these things, happy are you if you do them.

German (Erfurt)

> Christus: Szo ich ewre fuesze habe gewaschen der ich ewir herr vnd meyster bin / vill mehr solt yr einander vnter euch die fusze waschen. Hiemit habe ich euch ein antzeygung vnd beyspiel geben / wie ich ym than habe / alszo solt yr hinfur auch thuen. Warlich warlich sage ich euch / der knecht ist nicht mehr dan seyn herre / szo ist auch nicht der geschickte botte mehr dan der yn gesandt hat / Wist yr das? Selig seyt ir szo yr das thuen werdent. *Johan. 13.*

Christ: If I then, who is your lord and master, have washed your feet, so even more should you wash one another's feet. With this I have given you a demonstration and example that from now on you should also do as I have done to him. Verily, verily, I say unto you, the servant is not greater than his master; nor also is the dispatched messenger greater than he who sent him. Do you know this? Blessed are you if you will do so (John 13).

Commentary and linguistic comparison

The account is taken from the Gospel of John, in which Jesus washes his disciples' feet on Maundy Thursday. The German translates Latin *exemplum* (example) with two words: *ein antzeygung vnd beyspiel* (*a demonstration and example*). This perhaps reinforces the message of imitation. In the final sentence, while the Latin is phrased as a conditional clause (*If you know these things...*), the German uses a direct question (*Do you know this?*), to engage even more directly with the reader.

In the Strasbourg mirror copy of the woodcut, the gesture of wonder by the apostle whose feet are washed (Peter) is further exaggerated.

The washing of feet in the Wittenberg edition (left) and Strasbourg edition (right)

III 6: The pope has his feet kissed (A4r)

The pope sits on a raised throne with his hand lifted up in blessing and presents his foot to be kissed by a prince. Bishops, tonsured monks, nobles and princes surround the throne.

Latin

> Antichristus: Papa nititur imitari nonnullos tyrannos et ethnicos principes, qui pedes suos hominibus præbuerunt osculando. Ut verum fiat quod scriptum est: quicumque non adoraverit imaginem bestiæ occidatur. Apocalip. xiii [Rev 13:15]. De huiusmodi pedum osculatione non dubitat papa se impudenter in suis decretalibus iactitare. c. cum olim de privilegiis [Decretal., V 33 c. 12, CorpIC 2, 854]. cle. [I 10, c. 4. CorpIC 2, 1192] Si summus pontifex de sent. excom.

Antichrist: The pope endeavours to imitate several tyrants and heathen princes who display their feet to the people for kissing. So that it becomes true what is written: Whoever does not worship the image of the beast will be killed (Revelation 13). There is no doubt that the pope boasts of the kissing of the feet in this way shamelessly in his decretals (c. *cum olim* on privileges. Clementina. *Si summus pontifex* on the sentence of excommunication).

German (Erfurt)

> Antichristus: Der Babst mast sich an itzlichen Tyrannen vnd heydnischen fursten / szo yre fuesz den leuten tzu kuszen dar gereicht / nach tzuvolgen / damit es waer werde das geschriben ist. Wilcher dieser bestien bilde nicht anbettet / sall getôd werden. *Apocalip. 13.*
> Ditz kussens darff sich der Bapst yn seynen decretalen vnuorschembt rûmen. *c. cum olim de pri. cle. Si summus pon. de sen. excom.*

Antichrist: The pope presumes to imitate each of those tyrants and heathen princes who hold out their feet for the people to kiss so that it becomes true what is written: Whoever does not worship the image of this beast shall be killed (Revelation 13).

The pope may brazenly boast of this kissing in his decretals (c. *cum olim* on privileges. Clementina. *Si summus pontifex* on the sentence of excommunication).

Commentary and linguistic comparison

Luther had already made use of the opposition of Christ kissing and washing his disciples' feet and the pope having his feet kissed in *Nobility* [LW 44.1, 168]: "Further, the kissing of the pope's feet should cease. It is an un-Christian, indeed, an anti-Christian thing for a poor sinful man to let his feet be kissed by one who is a hundred times better than himself. If it is done in honour of his authority, why does the pope not do the same to others in honour of their holiness? Compare them with each other: Christ and the pope. Christ washed his disciples' feet and dried them but the disciples never washed his feet. The pope, as though he were higher than Christ, turns that about, and allows his feet to be kissed as a great favour."

The text combines an authorial intervention with both quotation from the Book of Revelation and two separate references to canon law. While under other papal images canon law is directly quoted, here the author(s) merely provide the references, the first to the *Decretals of Gregory IX*, known as the *Liber extra*, and to the title on privileges, i.e. exemptions from the law for specific purposes, and the second to the 1314 Constitutions of Clement and to the title on excommunication.

The German is a faithful translation of the Latin. The translation of *impudenter* with *vnuorschembt* picks up the use of the same word in I 2. The Strasbourg edition replaces *mast sich* (NHG: sich anmaßen) with *fleißt sich* (NHG: sich befleißigen).

IV 7: Christ and Peter pay customs (A4v)

Christ, at the left of the woodcut, gestures to the figure of Peter who is drawing out a coin from the mouth of a fish. An official bearing a purse walks out from an archway to meet him.

Latin

> Christus: Vade ad mare, et mitte hamum, et eum piscem, qui primus ascenderit, tolle, et aperto ore eius, invenies staterem. Illum sumens, da eis pro me et te. Matthei. xvii [Matt 17:23-26]. Reddito omnibus debita: cui tributum, tributum; cui vectigal, vectigal; cui timorem, timorem; cui honorem, honorem. Paulus ad Ro: xiii [Rom 13:7].

Christ: Go to the sea and cast a hook, and take up the first fish that comes up. And when you have opened his mouth, you will find a small silver coin inside. Taking this, give it to them for me and for you (Matthew 17). Render to all their dues: tribute to whom tribute is due; custom to whom custom; fear to whom fear; honour to whom honour (Paul to the Romans 13).

German (Erfurt)

> Christus: Gehe hyn tzum mehr / vnd laß yn dynen hamen / dem ersten fisch der sich vff wirfft / thue das mauel auff / dorinnen wirstu finden einen gulden / den gib tzu tzoll vor mich vnd dich. *Math. 17*
> Gebt der obirkeyt die das schwerdt in yren henden hat seyne gebüre / den tzinß / wem der tzinß tzustehet / den tzoll dez er gebürdt. *Paul. ad Roma. 13.*

Christ: Go to the sea and cast your hook. Open the mouth of the first fish which comes up. You will find a guilder inside, pay the toll with it for me and you (Matthew 17).

Render authority which wields the sword in its hands its dues; interest to him who is owed interest; the toll to him to whom it is due (Paul to the Romans 13).

Commentary and linguistic comparison

The Gospel of Matthew recounts how Jesus and his disciples arrived in Capernaum and the collectors of the temple tax came to Peter and asked whether his teacher had paid the temple tax. Peter replied in the affirmative and came to Jesus who asked: "From whom do the kings of the earth collect duty and taxes – from their own children or from others?" Peter replied "From others". Jesus responded that the children were exempt, but so as not to cause offense, Peter should go out and fish and would discover a coin in the first fish that he caught. Christ therefore commanded to pay the authorities their dues, echoed in the passage from Romans.

While the *Antithesis* quotes Rom 13:7, the *Passional* extends the quotation freely from Romans 13:4. Thus the passages on fear and honour are missing from the German. The German is, however, more expansive in its translation of *Reddito omnibus debita* (*Render to all their dues*) as *Gebt der obirkeyt die das schwerdt in yren henden hat seyne gebüre* (*Render authority which wields the sword in its hands its dues*), making it clear that the payments are for those yielding secular and military power.

The Strasbourg edition makes linguistic changes: as *hamen* was not used in southwestern Germany it was changed to *angel* [Kaufmann 2019:650, n. 872], while guilder (*gulden*) is replaced with a penny coin (*einen müntz pfennig*).

IV 8: The pope imposes the ban on authorities who tax the clergy (B1r)

The pope sits on a dais next to members of the clergy (monk, bishop, cardinal, canon). The pope hands down a sealed interdict to a group of princes. A group of clergy (nun, monk, two priests) walk towards the princes bearing sacks of money.

Latin

> Antichristus: Decernimus, qui iurisdictionem temporalem obtinent vel iusticiam secularem exercent, taleas, vel collectas seu exactiones quascumque ecclesiis vel personis ecclesiasticis imponere, vel exigere ab eisdem pro domibus, prædiis vel quibuscumque possessionibus, ab eisdem ecclesiis vel personis ecclesiasticis. c. i. De immunitate ecclesiarum[9], Liber Sextus [III 23 C. 1, CorpIC 2, 1061]. Sic papa suis mandatis mandata Dei dilaniavit. Id quod unicum est opus impiarum et antichristianarum decretalium eius.

Antichrist: We decree that [it is not permitted for][10] whomever has secular jurisdiction or exercises secular justice to impose any kind of tallage or contributions or taxes on the churches or clerical persons, or demand them from the same churches or ecclesiastical persons for

---

[9] ecclesiarum] *Ecle.*

[10] The Latin is a grammatically incomplete sentence as the quotation from the decretal was not copied over accurately, specifically the inclusion of the phrase *non licere*. The decretal reads: *decernimus, non licere praefatis communiis, scabinis, et iis, qui in eis iurisdictionem temporalem obtinent vel iustitiam temporalem exercent, tallias, vel collectas seu exactiones quascunque ecclesiis vel personis ecclesiasticis imponere, vel exigere ab eisdem pro dominubus, praediis vel quibuscunque possessioinibus, ab eisdem ecclesiis vel personis ecclesiasticis legitime hactenus acquisitis vel in posterum acquirendis, etiamsi ipsae ecclesiae vel personae vel res huiusmodi sint infra illorum distirctum vel territorium constitutae.*

their homes, manors or any kind of possessions (c. i. On the immunity of the churches, Liber Sextus). In this way the pope tears up God's laws by his laws. This is the sole work of his impious and antichristian decretals.

German (Erfurt)

> Antichristus: Wir setzen vnd ordnen das den mit nicht getzimen sall ßo den weltlichen gerichts zwangk haben stewir vnd schoß den geystlichen personen vfftzulegen ader den tzu forderen von yren hewsern vnd allen andern guttern bey der puß des schweren bans vnd interdictis / des gleychen sollen die geystlichen dieße alle nicht tzalen sonder vnßer erleubnis. *c.i. de immunit. eccle. li. vi.* Alßo hat der Babst gots gebot durch seyne gebott tzurissen / welchs seyner vnchristlichen decretael eynigs werck ist.

Antichrist: We order and decree that it shall not be appropriate for those who hold secular jurisdiction to impose taxes and contributions on clerical persons or to demand this from their houses and all other goods, on the pain of the ban and interdict. Equally the clergy should not pay all this without our permission (c. i. "On the immunity of the churches", Liber 6). In this way the pope has torn up God's laws by his laws, which is the sole work of his unchristian decretals.

Commentary and linguistic comparison

Immunities were exemptions established by law in favour of ecclesiastical property and clerics. While the *Antithesis* quotes from *Liber Sextus Decretalium* (the collection of decretals compiled under Pope Boniface VIII), the German adds significant extra information. First, that the pope orders the ban or interdict on those who levy tax on clerical persons or their property. Secondly, that the clergy should not pay tax without the permission of the papacy. While the German text describes the decretals merely as unchristian, the Latin describes them as both impious and antichristian.

V 9: Christ prays with the lame, lepers and blind (B1v)

Christ, holding his hand in prayer, and his disciples stand outside the city and meet a group of lame and sick people.

Latin

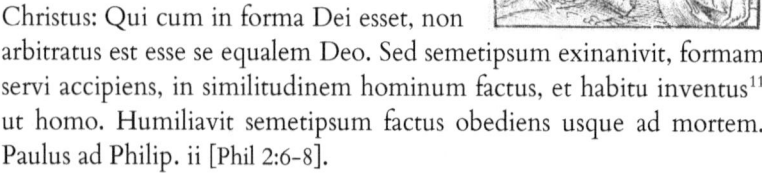

Christus: Qui cum in forma Dei esset, non arbitratus est esse se equalem Deo. Sed semetipsum exinanivit, formam servi accipiens, in similitudinem hominum factus, et habitu inventus[11] ut homo. Humiliavit semetipsum factus obediens usque ad mortem. Paulus ad Philip. ii [Phil 2:6-8].

Christ: Who, being in the form of God, did not think he was equal to God. But he emptied himself, taking on the form of a servant, was made in the likeness of men, and was found in appearance as a man. He humbled himself, and became obedient unto death (Paul to the Philippians 2).

German (Erfurt)

Christus: Christus aber wol yn der gotlichen form war / dennoch hat er sich des geewsert sich genydert vnd geberdet wie ein knecht gleich den andern menschen an tzusehen vnd befunden ein mensch der sich gedemütiget hatt / vnnd ist gehorsam geweßen biß in den todt. *Philippenses. 2.*

Christ: Although Christ took on divine form, he nevertheless divested himself of this, humbled himself and acted like a servant, appearing in the likeness of other men and found as a man who had humbled himself and he has been obedient unto death (Philippians 2).

---

[11] inventus] *innotus.*

Commentary and linguistic comparison

The extract from Paul's Letter to the Philippians does not refer to the woodcut directly, but rather emphasises Christ's humility in taking on the form of a servant. The word *rapinam* (robbery), which can be found in the Vulgate, is missing in the *Antithesis*, an indication that the author was either quoting freely or from memory or was even seeking to simplify the text for lay people by emphasising Christ's humility more strongly. The final phrase of Philippians 2:8, "even the death of the cross", is removed in both versions.

The German *aber* in the Erfurt edition is a typographical error for *ab er*: this is changed to *Wie wol* in the Strasbourg edition. The latter provides a shortened version, replacing the passage about his appearance as servant with a new phrase which cannot be found in the Erfurt edition, namely that Christ *lived among the poor and sick people (bey den armen krancken menschen gewondt)*. The intention was likely to make the association with the image even clearer.

Chꝛiſtus aber wol yn der gotlichen foꝛm war/ dennoch hat er ſich des geewſert ſich genydert vñ geberdet wie ein knecht gleich den andern menſchen an guſehen vnd befunden ein menſch der ſich gedemutiget hatt / vnnd iſt gehoꝛſam geweſen biß uꝛ den todt. Philippenſes. 2.

Erfurt (above) and Strasbourg (below) version of V 9

Wiewol Chꝛiſtus jn der gotlichen foꝛm war/ den noch hat er ſich des genydert/ vñ bey den arme kracke en menſchen gewondt/ſich ſelbs gedemutigt vnd ge=boꝛſam geſein vntz in todt. Philippenſes.2.

§ Wiewol Christus jn der gŏtlichen form war / dennoch hat er sich des genydert / vñ bey den armē krācken menschen gewondt / sich selbs gedemŭtigt vnd ge-horsam gesein vntz in todt. *Philippenses. 2.*

V 10: The pope presides over a knight's tournament (B2r)

The pope, wearing the tiara, sits on high with a retinue of clergy and watches over a jousting tournament between knights. Two heralds blow trumpets on the right, while a group of ladies look down on the left.

Latin

Antichristus: Papa putat sibi parum esse honorificum, si se humiliet. Dum enim nimium servatur humilitas regendi frangitur auctoritas[12]. lxxxvi. dist. c. Quando [Decr., d. 86 c. 4, CorpIC 1, 298]. Ubi dicit glosa [Decretum Gratiani [...], Lyon: Nicolaus de Benedictis, 12 May 1506, fol. 87rb]: Quod verum est inter fatuos. Hoc est, quatenus cum severitate imperandum est Germanis fatuis, tantum nobis tribuunt.

Antichrist: The pope considers it insufficiently honourable if he humbles himself. For if humility is served too excessively, then the authority of one's reign will be undermined (dist. 86, c. 4 *Quando*). As the gloss says: It is true among the fools. That is, with as much severity as the German fools must be governed, they grant as much to us in return.

German (Erfurt)

Antichristus: Der Bapst meynt es sey seynen ehren tzu nahe das er sich demůtige / dan der sich tzu fast demůtiget gedeyet yhm yn dem regiment tzuuorachtung. *c. quando 86. dist.*

---

[12] auctoritas] *autoritas.*

Alßo sagt die glosa / das ist waer bey den narren / das ist ßo vill man muß gestreng vbir die deutschen narren regiren / ßo halten sie vill[13] von vns.

Antichrist: The pope thinks that it would taint his honour to humble himself. Because he who humbles himself too much allows his reign to be undermined (dist. 86, c. 4 *Quando*).

Thus the gloss says: It is true among the fools, that is, you have to be strict with the German fools, then they will hold us in high esteem.

Commentary and linguistic comparison

The text begins with an authorial commentary, before quoting the *Decretum Gratiani*, which itself had its origins in the sixth chapter of the Rule of St. Augustine, on asking pardon and forgiving offenses. The text then introduces a nationalistic element for the first time, by suggesting that the pope must consider the Germans to be fools, to try to rule them as he does [Scribner 2004:151]. In the Strasbourg edition this is expressed differently. First, it notes how it is true *among the fools and ignorant (Das ist war bey den narren / vnnd vnuerstendigen)*. The first part of this was added as marginalia in the Pitts copy, along with further anti-papal sentiments.[14]

Secondly, it changes the final sentence: *That is, you have to be strict with the German fools, then they will hold our mandates and prohibitions, full of fear (Das ist souil / man můß streng über die teütschen narren regieren / so halten si vnser mandat vnd verbott inn forcht)*. The reworked sentence heightens the emotional aspect through the introduction of the word fear and emphasises the restrictive aspects of papal commands.

---

[13] vill] *veil*.

[14] On the marginalia in the Pitts copy cf. Ulrich Bubenheimer, Buying and Reading Anti-Papal Polemic (History of the Book blog, posted June 2021) https://historyofthebook.mml.ox.ac.uk/buying-and-reading-anti-papal-polemic/

Pitts Theology copy with antipapal marginalia, Bijr
Permalink: http://pid.emory.edu/ark:/25593/t9tnj

VI 11: Christ carries his cross (B2v)

Christ stumbles under the weight of the cross which is taken up by Simon of Cyrene, as the soldiers mishandle him. Note that in the first two Wittenberg editions of the *Passional* Jesus is shown walking barefoot with two disciples but that this woodcut was replaced in subsequent editions.

Latin

> Christus: Jesus fatigatus ex itinere, sedebat sic supra fontem. [John 4:6]. Si quis vult venire post me, abneget semetipsum, tollat crucem suam, et sequatur me. Matthei: xvi [Matt 16:24].
> Et baiulans sibi crucem exivit in eum, qui dicitur Calvariæ locus. Iohn xix. [John 19:17].

Christ: Jesus, being wearied from his journey, thus sat by the well (John 4). If anyone wants to come after me, let him deny himself, and take up his cross and follow me (Matthew 16). And bearing his cross he went forth to a place which is called Calvary (John 19).

German (Erfurt)

> Christus: Alß Jhesus ist eyn weytten wegk gangen / ist er můd worden. *Johan. 4.* Der mir will nach folgen / der nem seyn Creutz vff sich vnd folge mir. *Matthei 16.*
> Er hat ym seyn Creutze selbest getragen vnd ist tzu der stell die Caluarie genant wirdt / gangen. *19.*

Christ: When Jesus walked a long way he became tired. John 4. Whoever wants to imitate me must take upon himself his cross and follow me (Matthew 16).
He carried his own cross and went to the place which is called Calvary ([John] 19).

Commentary and linguistic comparison

Jesus sitting by Jacob's well in the *Antithesis* is excluded in the
Passional. The reference to John 19 was accidentally reduced to just
the chapter number in the German version.

The woodcut of Christ walking with the disciples in the first German edition,
Wittenberg 1521, VD16 L 5584 (copy BSB Res/4 H.eccl. 870,11)

VI 12: The pope is carried on a palanquin (B3r)

The pope, carrying a small crucifix, is carried on a palanquin or litter by a group of men. They come towards an archway bearing the papal coat of arms.

Latin

> Antichristus: Capitulum Si quis suadente diabolo [Decr., C. 17 q. 4 c. 29, CorpIC 1, 822] et similia satis superque probant, quam libenter papa crucem adversitatis toleret, cum omnes quicumque manus in sacerdotes iniciunt, maledict, et diabolo tradit. Sic etiam fert crucem papa, ut baptisati Christiani cogantur eum humeris suis portare.

Antichrist: The chapter "If anyone, having been persuaded by the devil" and the like demonstrate enough and more how willingly the pope endures the cross of adversity, when he curses all those who lay their hands on priests and hands them over to the devil. Thus the pope also bears the cross that baptised Christians are forced to bear him on their shoulders.

German (Erfurt)

> Antichristus: Das capittel *Si quis suadente* vnd der gleychen tzeygt gnug an wie gerne der Bapst das Creutz der wyderwertigkeyt duldet / so er alle die ihenen / die handt an die pfaffen an legen vormaladeyet vnd dem teuffel gibt Vnd alßo ouch tregt der Bapst das Creutz das ynnen getauffte Christen vff yren achsselen tragen mussen.

Antichrist: The chapter beginning "If anyone, having been persuaded" and the like sufficiently shows how gladly the pope endures the cross of adversity, when he curses all those who lay their hands on priests and gives them to the devil. And thus the pope also bears the cross of having to be carried by baptised Christians on their shoulders.

Commentary and linguistic comparison

Luther in *Nobility* once again has already made a similar comparison between Christ carrying his cross and the pope being carried [LW 44.1 pp. 168-169]: "Another example of the same scandalous pride is that the pope is not satisfied to ride or be driven, but, although he is strong and in good health, he has himself borne by men like an idol and with unheard-of splendour. Dear readers, how does such satanic pride compare with Christ, who went on foot, as did all his disciples? Where has there ever been a worldly monarch who went about in such worldly pomp and glory as he who wants to be the head of all those who ought to despise and flee from the pomp and vanity of this world, that is, the Christians? Not that we should bother ourselves very much about him as a person, but we certainly ought to fear the wrath of God if we flatter this sort of pride and do not show our indignation. It is enough for the pope to rant and play the fool in this way. But it is more than enough for us to approve of it and let it go on."

The canon in the *Decretum Gratiani* was issued at the Second Lateran Council (1139) and decreed that anyone who was violent towards a cleric or monk was excommunicated and that absolution could only be sought from the papal court. The canon therefore created a special immunity from violence in the clergy, in which the papacy acted as the guarantor of that immunity [Helmholz 1988].

In the German text *diabolo* is removed from the beginning of the quotation. Both versions merely cite the Incipit and do not provide the specific reference to canon law.

VII 13: Christ preaches to the people (B3v)

Christ stands in the countryside preaching to a group of men, women and children, some of whom are sitting on the ground.

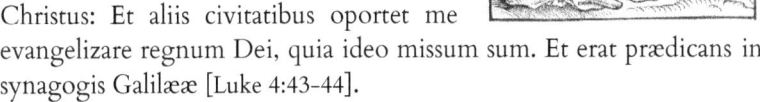

Latin

> Christus: Et aliis civitatibus oportet me evangelizare regnum Dei, quia ideo missum sum. Et erat prædicans in synagogis Galilææ [Luke 4:43-44].

Christ: And I must preach the kingdom of God to other cities because I have been sent for this purpose. And he was preaching in the synagogues of Galilee (Luke 4).

German (Erfurt)

> Christus: Jch muß auch andern steten predigen das reych gots / dan ich von deß wegen gesandt byn / vnd hab gepredigt in den Sinagogen durch Galileam *Luce. 4.*

Christ: I must also preach the kingdom of God to other cities, because I have been sent for this purpose, and have preached in the synagogues of Galile (Luke 4).

Commentary and linguistic comparison

Having healed Simon's mother-in-law from fever and people with various kinds of sickness, Jesus went to a solitary place at daybreak. The people looked for him and when they came to where he was, they tried to keep him from leaving them. His response is cited in the text. While the *Antithesis* is faithful to the Vulgate and places the second sentence in the third-person singular, the *Passional* adapts this and uses the first-person singular as if Jesus spoke this.

VII 14: The pope at a feast (B4r)

The pope sits drinking on a dais with a group of clerics and is brought food. A minstrel and fool stand in the background. A group of musicians stand in the foreground.

Latin

Sæpe contingit, quod episcopi propter suas occupationes multiplices, vel invalitudines corporales, aut hostiles incursus, aut occasiones alias, ne dicamus defectum scientiæ, quod in eis reprobandum est omino, per se ipsos[15] non sufficiunt ministrare verbum Dei populo, maxime per amplas dioceses et diffusas. Generali constitutione sancimus, ut episcopi viros ad sanctæ prædicationis officium salubriter exequendum assumant. c. Inter cetera de offi. ordina. [Decretal., I 31 c. 15, CorpIC 2, 192]. Hi sunt episcopi, qui ordinari officii sui obliti facti sunt animalia ventris [cf. Titus 1:12], dicentes: Venite, sumamus vinum, et impleamur ebrietate; et erit sicut hodie, sic et cras, et multo amplius. Esaie. lvi [Is 56:12].

It often happens that the bishops are not capable themselves of ministering the word of God to the people on account of their many obligations, or bodily sicknesses, or by hostile attacks, or other occasions, to say nothing of their lack of learning which is to be condemned by all. Particularly in the large and spread out dioceses we decree by general constitution that bishops take on men so that the office of holy preaching can be performed profitably (c. *Inter cetera* on the office of the priests). These are the bishops who have neglected their regular office and have become animals of the belly, saying: Come, let us take wine and become filled with strong drink; and it will be tomorrow as it was today, and much more abundant.

---

[15] se ipsos] *seipsos*.

German (Erfurt)

> Es geschicht offt das die Bischoff mit vielen hendlen beladen seyn / vnd von wegen yrer fheden / auch tzun tzeytten konnen sies nit / das dan nit seyn soll / mögen des predigens nit gewarten / sonderlich wan yre bistumb groß seint / dann mögen sie andere vor sich bestellen / die do predigen. *c. Jnter cetera de offi. ordina.* Das seynd die bischoff die yres ordentlichen ampts vergessen / sint worden animalia ventris. vnd sprechen / kommet vnd last vns schlemmen vnn temmen vnd alßo fur vnd fur gůt leben haben. *Esai. 56.*

It often happens that the bishops are burdened with many affairs, and, on account of their feuds, sometimes they cannot also provide preaching which should not be the case. Especially when their dioceses are large, then they may commission others to preach on their behalf (c. *Inter cetera* on the office of the priests). These are the bishops who forget their proper office, have become true "animals of the belly" and say: Come let us drink and feast and so live well the whole time (Isaiah 56).

Commentary and linguistic comparison

For reasons of space the German is shortened compared to the Latin, in particular the list of burdens affecting the bishops. In the Erfurt edition this is reduced simply to feuds, while in the Strasbourg edition more reasons are added: *because of the business of their domination, pomp, war and other incidences.* Whereas in the Erfurt edition, the causal connection is established between bishoprics being large and having to get replacement preachers, the first element is removed in the Strasbourg edition and need for replacements is explained by the list of reasons at the start.

The Latin quotes the decretal directly, but where the decretal describes the men to act as replacement preachers as *viros idoneos* (suitable men), the positive adjective is omitted in the *Antithesis*.

VIII 15: Birth of Christ in the stable (B4v)

Mary and Joseph kneel before the baby Jesus in a stable while the ox and ass look on. In the background the annunciation to the shepherds.

Latin

> Christus: Vulpes foveas habent, et volucres
> cæli[16] nidos. Filius autem hominis non habet ubi caput suum reclinet.
> Luce ix. [Luke 9:58].
> Scitis gratiam Domini nostri Jesu Christi, quoniam propter vos egenus
> factus est, cum esset dives, ut illius inopia vos divites essetis. ii. ad Corin.
> [2 Cor 8:9].

Christ: The foxes have their holes and the birds of the air their nests. But the son of man has nowhere to lay his head (Luke 9).
You know the grace of our Lord Jesus Christ, that, although he was rich, yet for our sakes he became poor, so that through his poverty you might become rich (2 Corinthians 8).

German (Erfurt)

> Christus: Die fůchß haben yre gruben / vnd die fogell der lufft yre
> nester / Aber der son des menschen hat nicht do er seyn heubt legte. *Lu.*
> *9.* Dießer ab er woll reich war / dennoch vmb vnsert willen ist er arm
> worden / vnd seyn armut hat vns reich gemacht. *2. Cor. 8.*

Christ: The foxes have their holes and the birds of the air have their nests. But the son of man has nowhere to lay his head (Luke 9).

---

[16] caeli] *coeli.*

Although he was rich, yet for our sakes he has become poor, and his poverty has made us rich (2 Corinthians 8).

Commentary and linguistic comparison

The phrase *You know the grace of our Lord Jesus Christ* (*Scitis gratiam Domini nostri Jesu Christi*) is omitted from the German translation.

In the Strasbourg edition, a stock woodcut is used for the nativity scene which means that the printer added an extra woodcut border to fit the block into the printing frame.

VIII 15 (B4v)

The Nativity in the Strasbourg edition, cf. below p. 75

VIII 16: The pope wages war (C1r)

The pope, wearing tiara and armour, stands before a group of foot soldiers and cavalry. While in all other woodcuts the pope is portrayed as fat, in this instance he is bearded and slim. This may refer to pope Julius II (1503-13), while the other woodcuts refer to Leo X (1513-21) [Dykema 2017:64, cf. images on p. 42].

Latin

> Antichristus: Absolvimus ab omnibus iuramentis et ne illa serventur vetuimus tam archiepiscopum Trevirensis, quam eius præpositum, et omnes, qui tunc temporis capti se illis quoquo modo obligaverunt etc. Hoc in mandatis damus, ut spirituali simul et materiali gladio tamdiu malignos illos eorumque fautores insequantur, quosque cum integritate possessiones, vel quæcumque res ecclesiasticæ hoc facto vel quocumque pacto distractæ vel direptæ sunt revocentur. c. Auctoritatem[17] xv. q. vi. [*Decr.* C. 15 q. 6 c. 2, CorpIC 1, 755]. Quisquis in hoc belli certamine fideliter mortuus fuerit, regna illi celestia minime negabuntur. 23. q. 5. c. Omnium [*Decr.*, C. 23 q. 5 c. 46, CorpIC 1, 944] et q. 8. c. Omni [*Decr.*, C. 23 qu. 8 c. 9, CorpIC 1, 955]. Novit omnipotens, si quilibet vestrum morietur, quod pro veritate fidei, et salvatione patriæ, ac defensione Christianorum mortuus est, et ideo ab eo præmium celeste consequetur. Scilicet hoc est, de suis rebus adeo certum esse, ut pro bonis habeantur, etiam si propter eas Christianus sanguis effundant.

We absolve from all oaths and, lest they are maintained, we prohibit them for the archbishop of Trier, as well as those placed under his command, and all those captured at that time who were bound to them in obligation in any way etc. We put this into law that they pursue with the spiritual as well as the material sword those evil ones

---

[17] Auctoritatem] *Autoritatem.*

and their supporters, and that they revoke their complete possessions or whatever ecclesiastical things which have been divided and laid to waste by this deed or whatever pact (c. *Auctoritatem*. xv. q. vi). And whoever dies faithfully in this contest of war, to him will the heavenly realms not be denied (23 q. 5. c. *Omnium* and q. 8. c. *Omni*). The almighty has learned that when one of you dies, he has died for the truth of the faith, the salvation of the patrimony, and the defence of Christianity. Therefore the celestial reward will follow from him. Namely it is so that one must be so sure of one's goods to consider them good even if on their account Christian blood is spilled.

German (Erfurt)

> Wir loßen auff alle eyde die die geystlichen tzu gefengknis gelobet haben vnnd gebietten das mann nit allein mit geystlichem / sonder auch mit dem weltlichem schwerdt yre gůter beschutzen sall / so lang biß das sie yr etwandt gutt widder haben *15. q. 6 c. Auctoritatem* / vnd der yn dießem krieck stirbt adir vordirbet wirt erlangen das ewig leben *23. q. 5. c. Omnium et q. 8. c. Omni* / das heyst seyns guts gewiß sein / das mans auch vor gut acht ob schon christen blůt daruber vorgossen wirdt.

We abrogate all oaths which the clerics have sworn in captivity and order that their goods should be protected not only by the spiritual but also by the worldly sword, until they have their former goods once again. *15. q. 6. c. Auctoritatem.* And whoever dies or perishes in this war will attain eternal life. *23. q. 5. c. Omnium et q. 8. c. Omni.* This means to be so sure of one's possessions that one regards them as good even though Christian blood is spilled because of them.

Commentary and linguistic comparison

In the first section of the passage the author(s) criticise the pope's right to release clerics who have been imprisoned by authorities from their oaths of obedience and the way in which he legitimises the defence of clerical goods with force. The first point in particular built on criticism already made by Luther. In *Why the Books of the Pope and His Disciples Were Burned*, he had criticised the pope as "he claims to have the power to dissolve all oaths, alliances, and obligations arranged between the higher and lower estates. This is against and above God, who ordered every man to keep faith with the other [Zech 8:16]" [LW 31.1:391]. Similarly in *Nobility* Luther had criticised that "they dissolve oaths, vows, and agreements, thereby destroying and teaching us to destroy the faith and fealty which have been pledged. They assert that the pope has authority to do this. It is the devil who tells them to say these things" [LW 44.1:193]. The *Antithesis* follows the original text of the decretal far more closely, not least by its inclusion of the reference to the archbishop of Trier.

The next section relates to an appeal made by Pope Leo IV (847-55) in 853 to the Frankish army to fight against Saracen marauders who had attacked Rome, including St Peter's, in 846, which was later integrated into canon law. The pope promised those who died in the battle eternal salvation [Brundage 1969:22]. Whereas the *Passional* only quotes one sentence, the *Antithesis* is more expansive and includes a further sentence.

The final section of the text adds a biting commentary that the pope is willing to spill Christian blood in his defence of clerical possessions.

The bearded pope (VIII 16, C1r) / Drawing by Raphael (?) of Pope Julius II
(Chatsworth House inv. no.757, ca. 1511)

IX 17: Christ rides into Jerusalem on a donkey (C1v)

Christ, holding up his hand in blessing, rides from right to left into Jerusalem on a donkey followed by its foal. The disciples follow behind on foot.

Latin

> Christus: Ecce rex tuus venit tibi mansuetus, sedens super pullum asine. Matthei. xxi. [Matt 21:1-8] et Iohann. xxi [John 12:14-15]. Sic venit Christus vectus asino alieno et mansuetus. Neque vectus est ad regendum et imperandum, sed ad beatam mortem nobis omnibus.

Christ: Behold your king comes unto you, meek, sitting upon the foal of a donkey (Matthew 21 and John 21). Thus comes Christ, meek, carried on a foreign donkey. For he was not carried to govern and to rule, but for a blessed death for us all.

German (Erfurt)

> Christus: Sich an / dein konigk kompt dir demütigk vff einem iungen esel *Mathei 21.* Alßo ist Christus kommen reyttendt vffinn frembden esel arm vnd sanfftmütigk vnd reydt nicht tzu regiren ßonder vns allen tzu eynem seligen todt *Johannis 12.*

Christ: Behold, your king is coming, lowly on a young donkey (Matthew 21). Thus has Christ come, riding on another's donkey, poor and gentle, and rides not to rule but for a blessed death for us all (John 12).

Commentary and linguistic comparison

On the one hand, the German is more economical, rendering *ad regendum et imperandum* (to govern and to rule) as *tzu regiren* (to rule). On the other hand, *mansuetus* is rendered as both *demütigk* and *arm vnd sanfftmütigk.* Christ's numerous qualities therefore come to the fore. The final phrase, that Christ rides not to rule but for our salvation, is not in the Vulgate.

The Strasbourg edition, by copying the original woodcut, changes the riding direction of both Christ and the pope.

IX 17 in the Erfurt edition and the Strasbourg edition

IX 18 in the Erfurt edition and the Strasbourg edition

IX 18: The pope rides into hell on a steed (C2r)

The pope rides on a steed at the head of a group of bishops and cardinals, following two foot-soldiers bearing halberds. The pope moves from left to right towards the mouth of hell. Hell waits at the back.

Latin

> Antichristus: Clerici omnes sunt reges, et hoc designat corona in capite. c. Duo xii. q. i. [Decr., C. 12 q. 1 c. 7, CorpIC 1, 678].
> Papa potest vehi instar imperatoris, et imperator debet stator[18] eius esse et frenum equi eius tenere, ut pontificalis apex non vilescat. 96. dist. c. Constantinus [Decr., d. 96 c. 14, CorpIC 1 344].
> Super gentes et regna pontifex Romanus a Domino constitutus. Extravaganti. Super gentes. Iohan. vicesimi secundi. [Extrav. com., 1 I c. 1, CorpIC 2, 1237]

Antichrist: The clergy are all kings, and this is designated by the crown on their head (c. *Duo* 12 q. 1).

The pope can be carried in the likeness of the emperor and the emperor ought to be his attendant and hold the reins of his horse so that the supreme pontificate does not become worthless (96. dist. c. *Constantinus*).

The Roman pontiff is established by the Lord above all peoples and kingdoms (Extravaganti *Super gentes*. John 22nd).

German (Erfurt)

> Antichristus: Die geystlichen seindt alle konnige vnd das betzeygt die platten vffim kopffe. *duo 12. q. 1.*
> Der Bapst magk gleich wie der keysser reytten vnd der keyser ist seyn

---

[18] stator] *strator.*

thrabant vff das bischofflicher wirden gehalt nicht gemindert werde. c. Constantinus. *96. dis.*

Der Bapst ist allen volckern vnd reychen vorgesatzt ex. vag. super gentes. *Johannis 22.*

Antichrist: The clergy are all kings, and this is shown by the tonsures on their heads (c. *Duo* 12 q. 1).

The pope may ride like the emperor and the emperor is his page so that the dignity of the bishop's status is not diminished. (96. dist. c. *Constantinus*).

The pope is placed above all the peoples and kingdoms. (Extravaganti *Super gentes.* John 22nd).

Commentary and linguistic comparison

The first reference to the *Decretum Gratiani* is taken from the separation of Christians into two distinct types: clerical and lay. Clerics are designated as kings, that is to say that they rule over others in virtues and thus have authority in God. *Corona* refers both to the crown but also tonsure.

The second quotation, similarly to II 4, is from the Donation of Constantine, which stated that a glittering tiara of dazzling white representing the Lord's resurrection was placed on his holy head, and that "holding the bridle of his horse, out of reverence for the Blessed Peter, we performed for him the duty of groom, decreeing that all his successors, and they alone, use this same tiara in processions in imitation of our power" [Valla 1922, pp. 16-17]. The Latin *pontificalis* (pontifical) is rendered as *bischofflicher* (episcopal) in German, creating a slightly different emphasis in meaning.

The final quotation from the *Extravagantes communes,* the set of papal decretals not found in Gratian's *Decretum* or the three official collections (*Decretals of Gregory IX, Sixth Book of the Decretals* and the *Clementines*), comes from a constitution that papal legates in all regions under papal authority must have absolute respect.

X 19: Christ sends out the disciples (C2v)

Christ stands outside among the disciples. At their feet lie a tunic and a bag. Peter takes off his belt with a purse and a disciple on the right is undressing. A city on a hill is visible in the background.

Latin

> Christus: Nolite possidere aurum, neque argentum, neque pecuniam in zonis vestris, non peram in via, neque duas tunicas, neque calceamenta, neque virgam. Matthei. x [Matth 10:9-10].
> S. Petrus dixit: Aurem et argentum non habeo. Actuum. iii [Acts 3:6]. Ubi est ergo patrimonium Petri?

Christ: Do not want to possess gold, nor silver, nor money in your belts, nor a bag for your journey, nor two tunics, nor shoes, nor a walking-staff (Matthew 10).
Saint Peter says: I have neither gold nor silver (Acts 3). Where is therefore the inheritance of Peter?

German (Erfurt)

> Christus: Jr solt nicht haben golt nach silber / nicht gelt an ewirn gorteln keyne taschen auch nit tzwen rôck noch schuch / nach eyn wanderstab. *Math. 10.*
> Sanct Peter sagt / Jch habe wyder golt nach silber Act. 3. *Vbi* ist dan *Patrimonium Petri?*

Christ: You should have neither gold nor silver; nor money in your belts, nor bags, nor two tunics as well or shoes or a walking-staff (Matthew 10).
Saint Peter says: I have neither gold nor silver (Acts 3). *Where* is therefore *the inheritance of Peter?*

Commentary and linguistic comparison

The first quotation comes from the Gospel of Matthew, in which Jesus has sent out the disciples and given them authority to drive out impure spirits and cure disease. They were to proclaim the message that the kingdom of heaven has come near.

The second quotation comes from the Acts of the Apostles. A lame person asks Peter and John who are about to enter a temple for money. Peter declares that he does not have gold or silver, but he gives what he does have, namely commanding the lame man to walk. The inclusion of Latin words in the Wittenberg and Erfurt editions indicates that the Latin text was written first. In the Strasbourg edition, *Vbi* is translated as *Wa*, and the word inheritance is included in both Latin and German (*Patrimonium vnd erbgůt*).

Jr ſolt nicht haben golt nach ſilber/nicht gelt an ewirn gorteln kcyne taſchen auch nit zwen rôck noch ſchu.h/nach eyn wan/ derſtab.Matth.10.
Sanct Peter ſagt/ Jch habe wyder golt nach ſilber Act.3.
Vbi iſt dan Patrimonium Petri?

Caption for X 19 in the Erfurt edition (above) and Strasbourg (below)

Jr ſolt nicht haben gold noch ſilber/ nicht gelt an ewern gůrteln/kein tåſchẽ/auch nit zwen rôck/noch ſchůch/noch ein wanderſtab.Mathei.10.
Sanct Peter ſagt. Jch hab weder goldt noch ſilber.
Act.3. Wa iſt dan Patrimonium vnd erbgůt Petri.

§ Jr solt nicht haben golt noch silber / nicht gelt an ewern gürteln / kein tåschẽ / auch nit zwen rôck / noch schůch / noch ein wanderstab. *Mathei. 10.*
Sanct Peter sagt. Jch hab weder goldt noch silber Act. 3.
Wa ist dañ Patrimonium vnd erbgůt Petri.

X 20: The pope shows a bishop a castle (C3r)

The pope stands with a group of clerics indoors, with a bishop at his left-hand side, pointing through an archway towards a town on a hill.

Latin

> Antichristus: Episcopi non in castellis
> neque in modicis civitatibus debent constitui, ne vilescat nomen
> episcopi, sed ad honorabilem locum titulandus est et denominandus
> episcopus. lxxx. dist. c. Episcopi [*Decr.*, d. 80 c. 3, CorpIC 1, 280].
> Sanctorum canonum statutis consona sanctione decernimus, ut sine
> titulo facta ordinatio irrita habeatur. lxx. dist. c. Sanctorum [*Decr.*, d. 70
> c. 2, CorpIC 1, 257].

Antichrist: Bishops ought not be confirmed in small fortresses and towns, lest it diminish the name of the bishop, but the bishop should be allocated and named to an honourable place (80 dist. c. *Episcopi*). We decree by harmonious decree to the statutes of holy canons that an ordination undertaken without title is considered void (70 dist. c. *Sanctorum*).

German (Erfurt)

> Antichristus: Keyn Bischoff sall auff eyn gering vnd kleyne stadt
> geweyet werden / sondern tzu eynem erlichen Titell gesatzt vnd hoch
> geehret seyn. *80. dist. c. Episcopi.*
> Wir ordnen das keyne wehung ane gnugliche vorsorgung krefftig sey.
> *70. dist. sanctorum.*

Antichrist: No bishop should be consecrated to an insignificant and small city, but rather be appointed and highly honoured with the title of an honourable place (80 dist. c. *Episcopi*).

We determine that no ordination without sufficient provision is valid. (70 dist. c. *Sanctorum*).

Commentary and linguistic comparison

While Christ demands poverty of his disciples whom he sends out into the world, the pope decrees that bishops should only preside over great towns and be given sufficient provision and appropriate honour.

The first reference begins with a direct quotation of the canon about bishops being appointed to small towns, but then adds an authorial comment, beginning *ne vilescat nomen episcopi* (lest it diminish the name of the bishop). This phrase is missing in the German translation.

The second quotation refers to the decree that forbade clerics from being ordained without a title, i.e. being ordained without having a specified church that he will serve and from which he will receive material and financial support. The canon which is quoted in the *Antithesis* was agreed at the Council of Piacenza (1095) [Wei 2016:275]. The German translation of *sine titulo* as *ane gnugliche vorsorgung* (*without sufficient provision*), makes clear that the emphasis was being placed on the aspect of material support. *Sanctorum canonum statutis consona sanctione decernimus* is rendered far more economically as *wir ordnen.*

Sanctorū Canonum ſtatutis conſona ſanctione decernimus , vt ſine ti-
ulo facta ordinatio irrita habeatur, lxx, diſt, c, ſanctorum.
                                                        C ij

The Latin version (above) and the shorter German (below) of X 20

Wir ordnen das keyne weyhung ane gnugliche vorſorgung
treffug ſey. 70.diſt.ſanctorum.   C iij

XI 21: Christ argues with the Pharisees (C3v)

Jesus is shown conversing with a group of men for whom a table in the foreground has been laid. A person from this group is already washing his hands. Disciples sit behind Jesus at a table which is already laid.

Latin

> Christus: Non veniet regnum Dei cum observatione, neque dicent: Ecce hic, aut ecce illic. Ecce enim regnum Dei intra vos est. Luce. xvii [Luke 17:20-21].
> Quare vos transgredimini mandatum Dei propter traditionem vestram? Sine causa colunt me, docentes doctrinas et mandata hominum. Matt. xv [Matt 15:1-3, 9] et Esaie. xxix [Is 29:13].

Christ: The kingdom of God will not come with observation. Neither will they say: See here, or see there! For behold the kingdom of God is within you (Luke 17).
Why do you transgress the commandment of God by your tradition? Those teaching human doctrines and laws are honouring me in vain (Matthew 15 and Isaiah 29).

German (Erfurt)

> Christus: Das reich gots ist nit yn ewsserlichen geberden / sie hie / aber do ist Christus / besonder das reich gots ist innerlich in euch. *Lu. 17.* Warumb habt ir das gebott gots vbirtretten von menschen gesetz wegern / Alle ehren mich vorgeblich / die do menschen lere vnnd gebott halten. *Mat. 15. Esaie. 21.*

Christ: The kingdom of God is not in outward signs, see here but there is Christ. Rather the kingdom of God is within you (Luke 17). Why do you transgress the commandment of God because of human laws? All who follow human teaching and commandments honour me in vain (Matthew 15, Isaiah 29).

Commentary and linguistic comparison

The first quotation from the Gospel of Luke is Jesus's reply to the Pharisees asking him when the kingdom of God would come. Jesus says that the coming of the kingdom of God is not something that can be observed. The sense of coming (*veniet*) is absent in the German, which simply uses the verb to be.

The final two sentences combine two quotations from the Gospel of Matthew (Matt 15:3, 9) with a passage from Isaiah which is not quoted. Image and text are not congruent. The image depicts Jesus discussing with the Pharisees their question why the disciples do not wash their hands before eating (Matt 15:1-3). One can only interpret the image by knowing this scene. In the text only Jesus's answer (Matt 15:3), extended by Matt 15:9, is included. Text and image therefore complement each other.

The Latin *propter traditionem* is rendered as *von menschen gesetz wegenn*, perhaps making even more explicit the contrast with canon law. In Latin the emphasis is on those teaching (*docentes*) human doctrines and laws, whereas in the German it is those following them (*halten*).

XI 22: The pope is worshipped by the clergy and people (C4r)

The pope sits on a throne on a dais as a group of praying figures, including a bishop, monks and nuns, stand and kneel before him.

Latin

> Antichristus: Antichristi regnum prorsus est in rebus exterioribus. Quid enim aliud dicit ius pontificum quam ordinationes de casulis, vestibus, coronis, festis, consecrationibus, beneficiis, sectis, ordinibus, monachis, et sacerdotibus. Et nominant, ut sese ita sua bona et facultates bona spiritualia, se solos ecclesiam catholicam, quasi vero prophani sive laici, necque in ecclesia sint, neque Dei, contra omnem scripturam. Præterea etiam prohibet cibos et matrimonium, quemdmodum Paulus ante prædexit: In novissimis temporibus discedent quidam a fide, prohibentium nubere, abstinere a cibis. 1. Timo. 4 [1 Tim 4:1, 3].

Antichrist: The kingdom of the Antichrist is completely in outward things. For what else does canon law speak of but of the ordering of chasubles, vestments, tonsures, feast days, consecrations, benefices, sects, orders, monks and priests? And they call their goods and powers spiritual goods; they say that they alone are the Catholic church as if truly the secular or lay folk were neither in the church nor or God, against all scripture. Additionally, he even prohibits meals and marriage, as Paul foretold: In the latter times some shall depart from the faith, forbidding marriage, abstaining from meat (1 Timothy 4).

German (Erfurt)

> Des Antichrists reich ist gantzlich in ewßerlichem weßen / was sagt des Bapsts recht anders den ordnung / von kaseln / cleydern / Platten /

feyertagen / weyungen / pfreunden / secten / monchen vnd pfaffen / vnd nennen sich / yr habe vnd gutter geystlich gutt / sich allein die Christlich kirche / die pfaffen dz außerwelt volck gots / gleich sam weren die leyen nicht in der kirchen vnd gots / widder alle schrifft / vbir das verbeut er die speyße / ehe / wie dan Paulus vorgesagt hat. Es werden kommen vorlogne geyst / vnd solche ding vorbieten. 1. Timo. 4.

The kingdom of the Antichrist is wholly of outward nature. For what else does canon law speak of except chasubles, vestments, tonsures, feast days, consecrations, benefices, sects, monks and priests? And they call their possessions and goods spiritual good, they call themselves alone the Christian Church, they call the priests the chosen people of God, as if the laity were not in the church and of God, contrary to all scripture. Additionally, he prohibits meals and marriage, as Paul predicted: There will come seducing spirits and forbid such things (1 Timothy 4).

Commentary and linguistic comparison

The first sentence of the text immediately makes clear the distinction between the inward nature of Christ and the outward nature of the Antichrist/pope. Despite referring explicitly to canon law, it does not directly quote or even refer to it.

The phrase that the priests are the chosen people of God is present in the German text but not in the Latin. This heightens the distinction between clerical and lay people.

The quotation from 1 Timothy 4 amalgamates two verses. In the Latin text, the author(s) quote the first part of the first verse, on those abandoning the faith. In the German text, however, the emphasis is placed on the seducing or deceiving spirits. The German text is then more economical, by not explicitly repeating the references to meat and marriage.

XII 23: Christ drives out the money changers from the temple (C4v)

Christ, bearing a whip, drives out a group of merchants, with a table turned over in the foreground. The disciples stand behind Christ.

Latin

Christus: Invenit in templo vendentes oves, et boves, et columbas, et numularios sedentes. Et cum fecisset quasi flagellum de funiculis, omnes ejecit de templo, oves quoque, et boves, et numulariorum[19] effudit aes[20], et mensas subvertit. Et his qui columbas vendebant, dixit: Auferte ista hinc, et nolite facere domum patris mei, domum negotationis.[21] Iohan. ii [John 2:14-16]. Gratis accepistis, gratis date. Matthei. x [Matt 10:8]. Pecunia tua tecum sit in perditionem. Act. viii [Act 8:20].

Christ: He found in the temple those that sold oxen and sheep and doves and the money changers sitting. And when he had made a whip out of cords, he drove them all out of the temple, and the sheep, and the oxen, and he scattered the changers' money and overturned their tables. To those who sold doves he said: "Take these out of here; and do not turn my father's house into a market!" John 2. Freely you have received; freely give. Matthew 10. May your money perish with you. Acts 8.

German (Erfurt)

Er hat funden ym tempel vorkauffer / schaff / ochßen vnd tawben vnd wechsler sitzen / vnd hat gleich eyn geyssel gemacht von stricken alle schaff / ochssen / tauben vnd wechßler außem tempell trieben / das gelt

---

[19] numularios /numulariorum] *nummularios / nummulariorum.*

[20] aes] *es.*

[21] negotationis] *negationis.*

verschůt / die tzall bredt vmkart vnd tzu den die tawben vorkaufften gesprochen. Hebt euch hin mit dießen auß meins vatern hauß / solt ir nit ein kauff hauß machen. *Joh. 2.* Jr habts vmb sunst / darumb gebts vmb sunst. *Mat. 10.* Dein gelt sey mit dir yn vordamnuß. *Act. 8.*

He found in the temple those selling sheep, oxen and doves and money changers sitting. And he soon made a whip out of cords and drove out all the sheep, oxen, doves and changers from the temple. He scattered the money, overturned the counting tables and to those selling the doves he said: Take these away. Do not make a market hall out of my father's house (John 2). Freely you have received; therefore freely give (Matthew 10). May your money be with you in damnation (Acts 8).

Commentary and linguistic comparison

The text recalls the story in the Gospel of John of Jesus driving the money changers from the temple. In the same way that Cranach's woodcuts sought to locate the scenes from the New Testament in the German present, the German translation also did so on occasion. The translation of *mensas* as *tzall bredt* is one such example.

A money table was used in the Middle Ages to aid counting, with lines cut into the table to represent ones, tens, hundreds and thousands. This is not depicted in Cranach's woodcut. Matthew 10:9 was already quoted in X 19, and this section quotes the verse before. The disciples are to heal the sick, raise the dead, cleanse the lepers and drive out demons. Jesus continues: Freely you have received; freely give. The final quotation from Acts concerns a story about a man named Simon who had practiced sorcery in Samaria. He was baptised by Philip. Peter and John were sent to Samaria and placed their hands on the believers so that they would receive the Holy Spirit. Simon offer Peter and John money to have the same ability. Peter replies with the phrase: "May your money perish with you, because you thought you could buy the gift of God with money!"

XII 24: The pope sits in church, selling sealed letters (D1r)

The pope sits on a throne on a dais signing sealed letters, with a group of clerics standing alongside. A number of people, including women, deposit money on a table, where a stack of letters is also placed.

Latin

> Antichristus: Hic sedet Antichristus in templo Dei, ostendens se tamquam sit Deus. Sicut Paulus prædexit. ii. ad Thessa. ii [2 Thess 2:4]. Commutat et subvertit omnes divinas constitutiones, quemadmodum Daniel dicit [Dan 11:36-37]. Opprimit sacram scripturam, vendit dispensationes, indulgentias, pallia, episcopatus, beneficia, tollit thesauros sæculi, dissolvit matrimonia, gravat suis legibus conscientias, sancit iura, et rursum eadem pro pecunia rescindit, refert in numerum divorum sanctos, sive canonizat, benedicit et maledicit in quartam generationem, et præcipit suam vocem audiri tamquam voce Dei. c. Sic omni dist. xix. [Decr., d. 19 c. 2, CorpIC 1, 60]. Et nemini est permissum de sedis apostolicæ iudicio iudicare vel retractare. xvii. dist. iiii. c. Nemini [Decr., C. 17 q. 4 c. 30, CorpIC 1, 823].

Antichrist: Here sits the Antichrist in the temple of God, presenting himself as God. As Paul foretells (2 Thessalonians 2). He alters and overturns all divine orders, as Daniel says. He suppresses holy scripture, sells dispensations, indulgences, pallia, bishoprics, benefices. He raises up the treasures of the world, dissolves marriages, burdens consciences with his laws, makes laws and tears them up again for money. He raises saints into the divine number, or canonises, blesses and curses unto the fourth generation and orders his voice to be heard just like God's voice (c. *Sic omni*, dist. 19). And nobody is permitted to judge or retract from the judgement of the apostolic seat (17 dist. 4 c. *Nemini*).

German (Erfurt)

Hie sitzt der Antichrist ym tempell gots vnd ertzeygt sich als got wie
Paulus vorkundet. *2. Tessal. 2.* vorandert alle gotlich ordnung / wie
Daniel sagt / vnnd vnterdruckt die heylig schryfft / vorkeufft
dispensacion / Ablas / Pallia / Bisthum / Lehen / erhebt die schetz der
erden / lôst auff die ehe / beschwerdt die gewissen mit seynen gesetzen /
macht recht / vnnd vmb gelt tzureyst er das / Er hebt heyligen /
benedeyt vnd maledeyet yns vierde geschlecht vnd gebewt sein stym
zuhôren / gleych wie gots stym. *c. sic omnis. dist. 19.* vnd niemants sall
ym eynreden. *17. q. 4. c. Nemini.*

Here sits the Antichrist in the temple of God and presents himself as
God, as Paul foretells (2 Thessalonians 2). He alters all the divine
order, as Daniel says, and suppresses holy scripture, sells
dispensations, indulgences, cloaks, bishoprics, benefices. He raises up
the treasures of the earth, dissolves marriages, burdens consciences
with his rules, makes legislation and tears it up again for money. He
raises saints, blesses and curses unto the fourth generation, and orders
his voice to be heard just like God's voice. (c. *Sic omni*, dist. 19). And
no one should argue against him (17 dist. 4 c. *Nemini*).

Commentary and linguistic comparison

The German translation is more economical and shortens some
elements: *commutat* et *subvertit* is rendered by *vorandert*, *refert* in
numerum divorum sanctos, sive canonizat by *Er hebt heyligen* and *Et
nemini est permissum de sedis apostolicæ iudicio iudicare vel retractare* by
vnd niemants sall ym eynreden.

In Paul's second letter to the Thessalonians, he writes about the
coming of a man of lawlessness who "will oppose and will exalt
himself over everything that is called God or is worshipped, so that
he sets himself up in God's temple, proclaiming himself to be God."
The passage quoted from the Book of Daniel is used to support this,
about a king who will exalt and magnify himself above every God.

The first reference to the *Decretum Gratiani* refers to a statement by pope Agatho that one should deem all laws of the apostolic seat as if they were confirmed by the divine voice of St Peter: "Sic omnes apostolicæ sedis sanctiones accipiendæ sunt, tanquam ipsius uoce diuina Petri firmatæ." In the *Antithesis figurata* this is adapted by the author(s) to refer to God's voice more generally.

The final quotation relates to the idea, widespread in canonical sources in the eleventh and twelfth century, that no one could judge the decisions of the pope.

In the set of images used for the Wittenberg edition, there is additionally a dog in the bottom left-hand corner which indicates that the selling of papal bulls or indulgence letters was qualified as particularly devilish. It has not been copied in the newly cut set for the Erfurt edition. The Strasbourg edition replaces it with a dragon as part of the ornamental border for the pope's throne.

Bottom left-hand corner of XII 24 in the Wittenberg editions, here taken from the Bodleian copy of the Latin edition, Douce C 313, D1r (left), the empty space in the Erfurt edition (right), and the dragon in the Strasbourg version (below).

XIII 25: Christ ascends to heaven (D1v)

Christ ascends to heaven, his right hand making a gesture of blessing and in his left hand holding a flag with the figure of the cross. He is accompanied by cherubim on clouds. He leaves his footprints behind on the mountain, a sign of his human nature. A group of men and women gaze up towards toward him on the left, with a city depicted on the right.

Latin

> Christus: Videntibus illis, elevatus est. Hic Jesus, qui assumptus est a vobis in cœlum, sic veniet quemadmodum vidistis eum euntem in cœlum. Act. 1 [Act 1:9,11]. Regni eius non erit finis. Luce 1 [Luke 1:33]. Si quis mihi ministrat, me sequatur, et ubi sum ego, illic et minister meus erit. Iohan. 12 [John 12:26].

Christ: While they watched, he was taken up. This same Jesus, who has been taken from you into heaven, will come back in the same way you have seen him go into heaven (Acts 1). There will be no end to his kingdom (Luke 1). Whoever serves me, follows me, and where I am, my servant will be (John 12).

German (Erfurt)

> Jn yren ansehen ist er auffgehaben vnd die wolcken haben ynn hinwegk genomemn von yren ougen. Dißer Jesus der von euch yn himmel auffgenommen ist / wirdt alßo wyder kommen wie yr ynn gesehen habt czu himmel fharen. *Act. 1.* Seyn reych hat keyn ende *Luce. 1.* Wer do mir dient der wird mir nach volgen vnd wu ich bin do wirt meyn diener ouch ßeyn. *Johan. 12.*

While they watched he was taken up, and the clouds took him out of their sight. This Jesus, who was taken up from you into heaven, will come again in the same way as you have seen him go into heaven (Acts 1). His kingdom has no end (Luke 1). Whoever serves me, will follow me; and where I am, there my servant will also be (John 12).

Commentary and linguistic comparison

The first quotation is an amalgamation of two verses from the opening chapter of Acts. The *Passional* adds the phrase about the clouds which is not present in the *Antithesis figurata*: *die wolcken haben ynn hinwegk genomemn von yren ougen*. This helps to create an even closer link with the depiction of the scene in the woodcut.

The second quotation is from the Gospel of Luke and how the birth of Jesus will be foretold.

The final quotation is from the Gospel of John and the moment when Jesus predicts his death. The final part of the verse, that "My father will honour the one who serves me", is omitted.

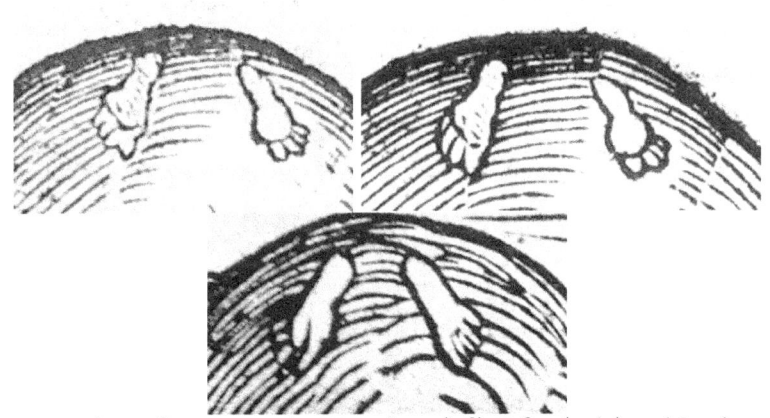

XIII 25: Christ's footprints in the Wittenberg (left), Erfurt (right), and Strasbourg (bottom) editions

XIII 26: The pope descends to hell (D2r)

The pope, wearing his crown and chasuble, is cast down into the flames of hell by a group of demons. He joins a group of lost souls, including a tonsured monk.

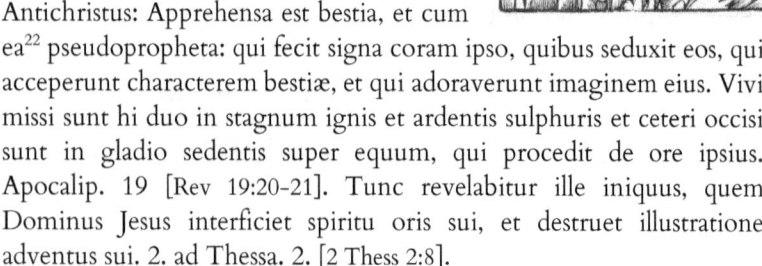

Latin

Antichristus: Apprehensa est bestia, et cum ea[22] pseudopropheta: qui fecit signa coram ipso, quibus seduxit eos, qui acceperunt characterem bestiæ, et qui adoraverunt imaginem eius. Vivi missi sunt hi duo in stagnum ignis et ardentis sulphuris et ceteri occisi sunt in gladio sedentis super equum, qui procedit de ore ipsius. Apocalip. 19 [Rev 19:20-21]. Tunc revelabitur ille iniquus, quem Dominus Jesus interficiet spiritu oris sui, et destruet illustratione adventus sui. 2. ad Thessa. 2. [2 Thess 2:8].

Antichrist: The beast was captured, and with him the false prophet, who performed signs on its behalf. With these signs he seduced those who had received the mark of the beast and worshipped his image. The two of them were thrown alive into the fiery lake of burning sulphur. And the rest were killed with the sword coming out of the mouth of the rider on the horse (Revelation 19). Then the unjust one will be revealed, whom the Lord Jesus will overthrow with the breath of his mouth and destroy by the splendour of his coming (2 Thessalonians 2).

German (Erfurt)

Antichristus: Es ist ergriffen die Bestia vnd mit yr der falsch prophet der durch sie tzeychen than hat / do mit er vorfurdt hat / die do seyn tzeychen von ym genommen / vnd sein bildt angebet ßeynt versenckt

---

[22] ea] *eo.*

yn die teuffe des fewirs vnd schweffels vnd seynd getodt mit dem
schwerdt des der do reydt vffim weyssen pferdt / das auß seynen mauel
gehet. *Apocal: 19.* Danne wirdt offenbar werden der schalckhafftige
denn wirdt der herr Jesus toeten mit dem atem ßeyns mundts vnd wirdt
yn sturtzen durch die glori ßeyner tzukunfft. *2. ad Tessa. 2.*

Antichrist: The beast was captured along with the false prophet, who
had performed signs on its behalf. With these he deceived those who
received his sign and worshipped his image; they have sunk into the
depth of the fire and sulphur and are killed with the sword that came
out of the mouth of the rider on the white horse (Revelation 19).
Then the lawless one will be revealed, whom the Lord Jesus will kill
with the breath of his mouth and overthrow by the glory of his
coming. (2 Thessalonians 2).

Commentary and linguistic comparison

The first quotation is taken from the passage in Revelation when the
heavenly warrior defeats the beast.

The reference to Paul's Letter to the Thessalonians builds on XII 24.
The passage would become an important part of Reformation
treatments of the Antichrist. An anonymous pamphlet printed in
1521, *A Dialogue between Two Good Friends named Hans Tholl and
Claus Lamp, talking about the Antichrist and his Followers* [Schade 1857],
tells of Hans attending a Bible-reading meeting. He has momentous
news to convey to Klaus and when he quotes verses from Paul's
Letter to the Thessalonians, Klaus exclaims in great amazement that
the pope must be the Antichrist.

Postscript (D2v)

Latin

> Cum autem famosus libellus dici non possit, nisi complectatur in se crimina et maleficia, manifestum est hunc libelllum pro famoso haberi non posse, neque sub edictis contra famosos libellos editis prohibitum esse. Cum omnia qui in hoc insunt libello, in pontificio spirituali iure, non solum tamquam licita, sed etiam tamquam leges et canones inveniantur. Est autem hic libellus hoc potissimum nomine editus, tantum ad notificandum breviter, fundamentum spiritualis carnalis iuris, precipue pro communi et publica utilitate totius Christiani orbis.
>
> Hæc æqui bonique consulite,
> Brevi meliora sequentur.

Since however a pamphlet cannot be called libellous unless it contains slanders and deceptions, then it is clear that this pamphlet cannot be considered libellous, nor can it be prohibited in the published decrees against libellous pamphlets. Since everything which is in this pamphlet can be found in papal canon law, not only as something permitted, but even as laws and canons. This pamphlet has however been chiefly published by name, to demonstrate things briefly on the basis of spiritual, carnal law, especially for the communal and public use of the entire Christian world.

Reflect on its fairness and goodness,
Shortly better ones will follow.

German (Erfurt)

> Sint eyn itzlich schandt buch / vnd *famosus libellus* nit mag genendt werden / es begreyfft dan yn sich schandtlich laster vnd vnthate / ßo ist offentlich / dz ditz buchle nit mag vor ein schandt buch gehalten werden / nach durch die gebot so widder die schand schrifft auß gangen / vorbotten sein / dieweyl alles das hirinnen steht / yn dem Bepstlichem geystliche rechte / nit allein als tzimlich dingk / ßonder

auch als gesetze tzubefinden / vnnd ist vornemlich außgangen / allein deß geystlichen / fleyschlichen rechts grundt yn eyner summe vnnd kurtzlich antzuzeygen gemeynem nutz der Christenheyt forderlich tzu gutte.

Nembt allßo vor gutt /
Es wirdt baldt besser werden.

If not every pamphlet can be called libellous, unless it contains within it libellous vices and misdeeds, so it is clear that this little book cannot be considered libellous nor be prohibited in the laws which have gone out against libellous writings. Since everything which is in it can be found in papal canon law, not simply as something tolerable, but rather as laws. And in particular it has been published solely to show the basis of spiritual and temporal law as a summary and in brief, conducive to the general benefit of Christianity.

Consider it therefore good,
There will soon be better ones.

Commentary and linguistic comparison

The postscript in both the Latin edition and the Wittenberg/Erfurt German editions emphasises from the outset that the pamphlet cannot be considered libellous nor be prohibited in light of recent laws against libellous publications. Kaufmann suggests this might refer to either the *Sequestrationsmandat*, promulgated by Emperor Chalres V on 10 March 1521 in which Luther's works should be retracted and destroyed, or to the Edict of Worms (25 March 1521). It is interesting to note that a plural form is used in both Latin and German (*edictis*; *die gebot*) so we should not rule that it refers to both of these. As Kaufmann notes, the fact that it was printed on the empty back page (D2v) means it could have been added quickly. He adds that the inclusion of the postscript may have been a further way of camouflaging the true intention behind the work. Indeed, in the last sentence, the postscript emphasies that this is both a short work and also beneficial for all of Christianity [Kaufmann 2019:651-2].

The two lines of verse refer to the fact that future publications are forthcoming, a reference, Kaufmann suggests, to either Melanchthon's Latin translation of Luther's *Von den guten Werken* (*On Good Works*) or Melanchthon's *Apologia* (*Apology*) for Luther against the attacks of the Paris theologians [Kaufmann 2019: 651, n. 877].

The Strasbourg editions print this text, but then add significant extra details to its postscript. First, an eight-line poem is appended, which states that the aim of the book is to clarify whether the pope is the Antichrist. Secondly, a fictional colophon is added, stating that *I have been printed in Noah's ark.* This seems to have been a humorous way for the printer Prüss to get round restrictions imposed by the Edict of Worms against the printing of such material [Kaufmann 2019: 652].

2. Facsimile, edition and translation

of the expanded edition Strasbourg 1521,
Bodleian, Tr. Luth. 250a

¶ Passional Christi vnd Antichristi.

Christus.
¶ Petre/ wan würd entbunden ich?
Wie lang verfolgt der Babst doch
mich?

Petrus.
¶ Jetz / so Babst Leo mit seim gesind.
Mit offenen augen ist starblind.

☞ Bapst
Stond nackent / beyd on dach ellend
Wardt biß ich eüwer armůt wend.
In gewalt / eer / reichtumb /
hochbrachtlich
Bezwing ich erd / vnnd himelrich.

Translation

Passional of Christ and Antichrist.

Christ: O Peter, when might I be released?
How long is the pope going to persecute me for?

Peter: Now there is Pope Leo with his entourage.
With eyes open, he is purblind.

Pope: Stand naked, both wretched and without a roof,
Wait until I reverse your poverty.
In power, honour, riches
Ostentatiously I conquer earth and the kingdom of heaven.
Christ: O Peter, when might I be released?
How long is the pope going to persecute me for?

I: The Kingdom (A1v–A2r)

Christus flog das irdisch Reich. ☞ Nûn zeichts der Bapst mit gewalt an sich.

Regna fugit Christus. Præsulque suscipit vrbis.

Translation

Christ fled the earthly kingdom. Now the pope pulls it with violence to himself.

Christ fled the kingdoms. And the bishop of the city seized them.

II: The Crown (A2v–A3r)

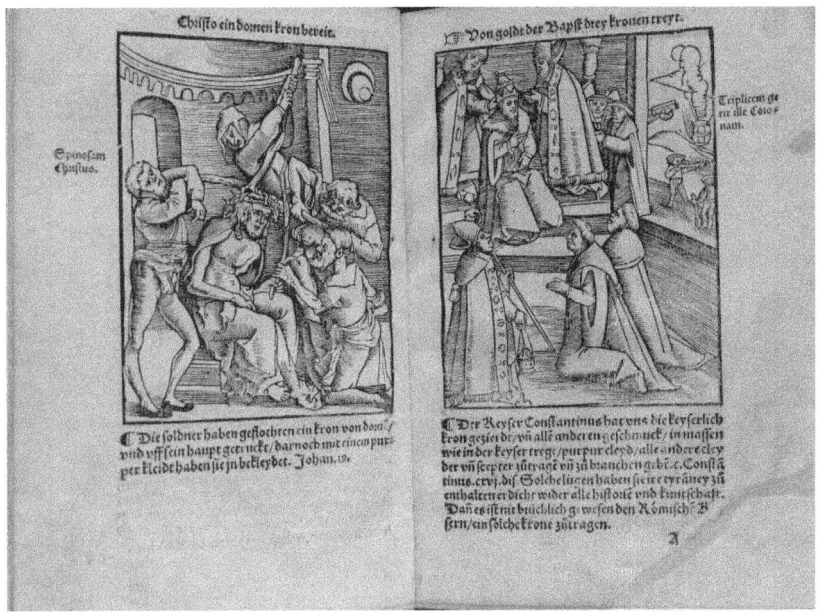

Christo ein dornen kronen bereit. ☛ Von goldt der Bapst drey kronen treyt.

Spinosam Christus. Triplicem gerit ille coronam.

Translation

A crown of thorns ready for Christ. The pope wears a triple crown of gold.

Christ wears a thorny crown. He wears a triple crown.

III: Washing or Kissing the Feet (A3v–A4r)

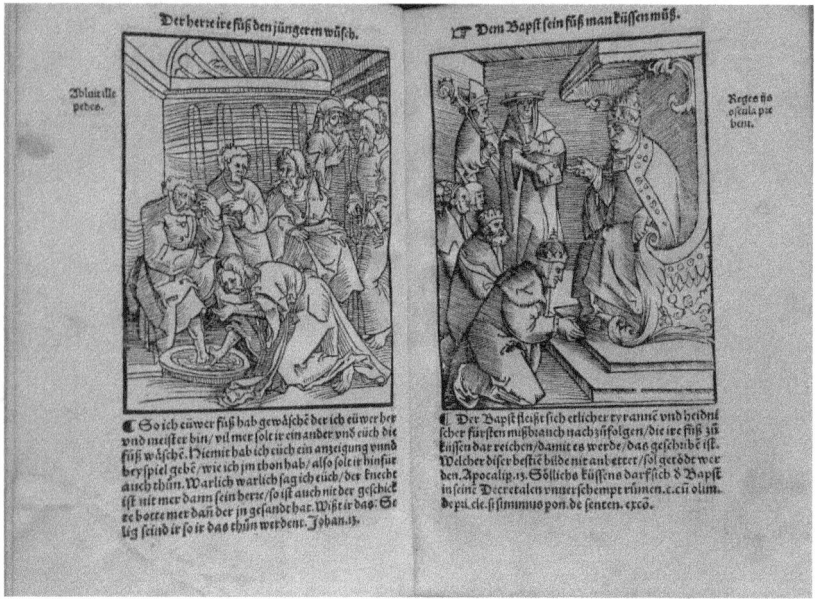

Der herre ire füß den jüngeren wůsch. ☛ Dem Bapst sein füß man küssen můß.

Abluit ille pedes. Reges iis oscula prebent.

Translation

The Lord washes the disciples' feet. One has to kiss the pope's foot.

He washes feet. The kings offer them [the feet] kisses.

IV: Paying Tax (A4v-B1r)

Selbs zinß vnd zoll der herr hat geben. ☞ Des wil gantz frey der Bapst yetzt leben.

Vectigal soluit. Sed clerum ille eximit omnem.

Translation

Even the Lord has given interest and toll. The pope wants to live quite freely from it.

He pays tribute. But he releases the whole clergy from it.

V: Caring for the Poor and Powerful (B1v–B2r)

Christus in demůt wonet bey den armen. ☞ Schampt sich der Bapst das ist zů erbarmen.

Pauper erat. Sed dives hic irradiantibus armis.

Translation

Christ lives with the poor in humility. The pope is ashamed of doing so. That is to be pitied.

He was poor. But this man is rich with shining weapons.

VI: Carrying the Cross and the Palanquin (B2v–B3r)

Offt Christum das Creütz zur erden truckt. ☞ Hie laßt sich tragen der Babst geschmuckt.

Baiulat ille crucem. Hic servis portatur avaris.

Translation

The cross pressed Christ often to the ground. Here the pope lets himself be carried in his finery.

This one [Christ] carries the burden of the cross. While this here [the pope] is carried by greedy servants.

VII: Preaching and Feasting (B3v–B4r)

Christus hat selbs sein schäflin geweydt. ☞ In wollust lebt dyser vnd üppigkeit.

Pavit oves Christus. Luxum hic sectatur inertem.

Translation

Christ himself has pastured his lambs. This man lives in lust and luxuriance.

Christ feeds the sheep. This here [the pope] seeks out worthless luxury.

VIII: Low and High Status (B4v–C1r)

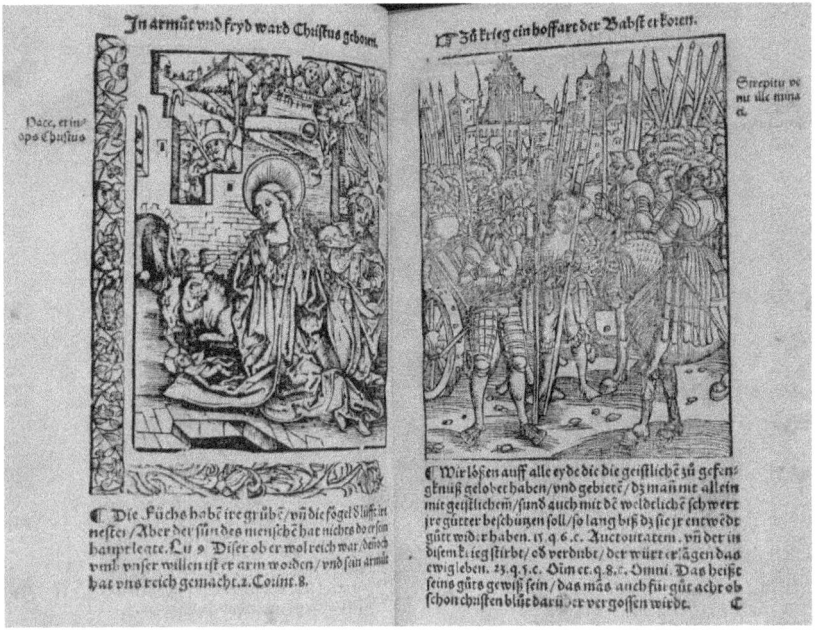

Jn armůt vnd fryd ward Christus geboren. ☞ Zů krieg ein hoffart der Babst erkoren.

Pace et inops Christus. Strepitu venit ille minaci.

Translation

Christ was born in poverty and peace. In war the pope has chosen pride.

Christ in peace and poor. This one [the pope] comes with threatening noise.

IX: Humility and Pride (C1v–C2r)

Senfftmüetig der herr kam geritten. ☞ Der Bapst in hoffart vnnd stoltzem sytten .

Christus mansuetus venit. Venit ille superbus.

Translation

The Lord gently came riding. The pope with arrogance and a proud manner.

Christ comes meekly. This one [the pope] comes proudly.

X: Poverty and Wealth (C2v–C3r)

Christus keins eygens noch golds bedurfft. ☞ Alle land der Bapst im vnder würfft.

Ille caret nummis. Regna hic tenet omnia mundi.

Translation

Christ has no need of either possessions or gold. The pope subdues all lands.

This one [Christ] is lacking coins. This here [the pope] holds all the kingdoms of the world.

XI: Internal and External Kingdoms (C3v–C4r)

Christus nichts hielt vff vsserliche berden. ☞ Hat gantz vmbgewendt der Bapst vff erden.

Quas leges dedit is. Præsul dissoluit iniquus.

Translation

Christ sets no store on external gestures. The pope has inverted everything on earth.

The unjust bishop revokes the laws which he has given.

XII: Rejecting or Collecting Money (C4v–D1r)

Die wůcherer Christus vßtreib vom tempel sein. ☞ Mit bullen banbriefen zwingt sy der Bapst wider hienin.

Vendentes pepulit templo. Quos accipit ille.

Translation

Christ drives the usurers from his temple. With bulls and letters of excommunication the pope forces them back inside.

He drove the traders from the temple whom he receives.

XIIA: Living in Poverty or Wealth (D1v–D2r)

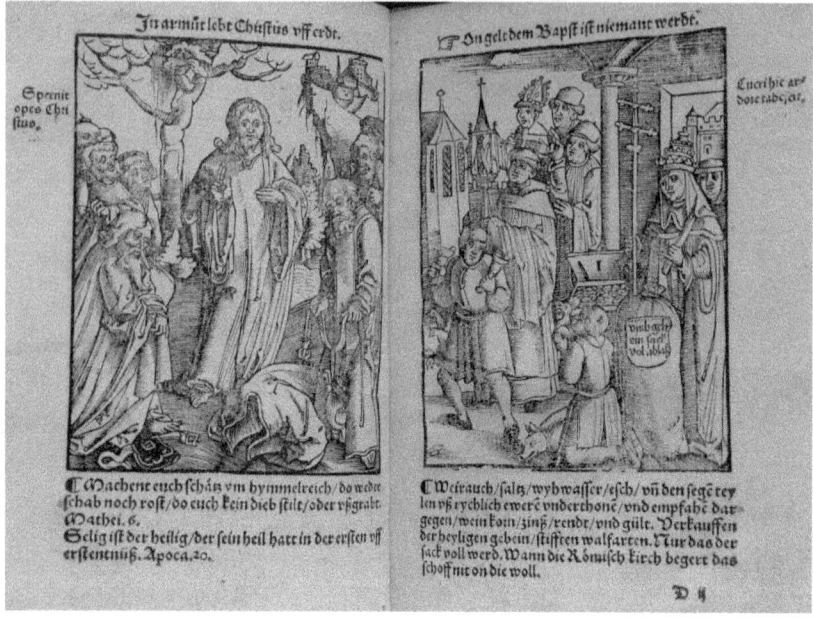

Jn armůt lebt Christus vff erdt. ☞ On gelt dem Bapst ist niemant werdt.

Spernit opes Christus. Lucri hic ardore tabescit.

Translation

Christ lives in poverty on earth. Without money nobody is worth anything to the pope.

Christ rejects wealth. He wastes away from his dependence on profit.

German text left

Machent euch schåtz vm hymmelreich / do weder schab noch rost / do euch kein dieb stilt / oder vßgrabt. Mathei. 6.
Selig ist der heilig / der sein heil hatt in der ersten vff erstentnüß. Apoca. 20.

Store for yourselves treasures in heaven, where there are neither cockroach nor rust, where no thief steals from you or digs it up. [Matt 6:20]. Blessed is the holy one, who has his salvation in the first resurrection. [Rev 20:6].

German text right

> Weihrauch / saltz / wyhwasser / esch / vnd den segen teylen vß rychlich eweren vnderthonen / vnd empfahen dar gegen / wein korn / zinß / rendt / vnd gült. Verkauffen der heyligen gebein / stifften walfarten. Nur das der sack voll werd. Wann die Rômisch kirch begert das schoff nit on die woll.

Incense, salt, holy water, ashes and blessings are all richly handed out to your subjects and in return they receive wine, corn, interest, income and revenues. They sell sacred bones and establish pilgrimages. Only so that the sack becomes full. Since the Roman church does not desire the sheep without the wool.

Commentary

This is the first of the two antitheses which the Strasbourg edition adds which, similarly to X, emphasises Christ's poverty. The left woodcut reuses X 19, the right shows the pope, with a cardinal behind, standing before a sack with the inscription *a sack of indulgences for money (vmb gelt ein sack vol ablaß)*. A man kneels down before a procession of clergy, including a monk holding a monstrance. A man at the front of the processions rings bells in both his hands to mark the procession.

This is the only text not to contain a biblical quotation or a reference to canon law. Instead the author(s) direct their ire towards the way in which resources are extracted, solely for the greed and wealth of the Pope.

XIIB: Grazing or Devouring Sheep (D2v–D3r)

Christus sein scheflin / weit trewlich. ☞ So frißts der wolffs bapst grausamklich.

Pascit oves Christus. Inopis hic sanguine gaudet.

Translation

Christ grazes his lambs truly. While the wolf pape gorges them cruelly.

Christ feeds the sheep. He [the pope] rejoices in the blood of the poor.

German text left

Jch bin ein gůter hirt / gang meinen schåflin vor / ston bey inen / weyd sie / setz mein seel für sie / vnnd ob schon der wolff kumpt / so verlaß ich sie nit / wan ich nit ir taglôner bin. Joh. 10. Grôsser liebe hat niemant / dann so einer sein seel für seine freünd setzt. Joh. 15.

I am a good shepherd, going before my sheep, stand next to them, pasture them, lay down my soul for them, and although the wolf comes, I do not abandon them, because I am not their hired hand. [John 10:4,11-13] Greater love has no one than this to lay down one's life for one's friends. [John 15:13].

German text right

> Habent acht vff die falschen propheten / bekleidt mit schaff wol / von jnen zuckend wölff. Lond vns den armen drucken / quetschen / tödten vnd fressen / im grosse bürdy vff legen / die wir nit mit eim finger anrürren. Math. xxiii. Der leyen verderbnüß / vnser herrlicheit.

Beware of false prophets, clothed with sheep's wool, inwardly ravening wolves. Let us press, crush, kill and eat up the poor, lay on them great burdens which we do not touch with a finger. [Matt 23:4]. The laypeople's disaster is our splendour.

Commentary

The second additional pair of images. On the left, Christ holds a lamb on his shoulders while another approaches his bare feet. A group of men, some with their hands in the gesture of prayer, gather around him. Image and text work as one to emphasise the nurturing nature of Christ. On the right, the Pope is presented as a wolf wearing the papal tiara and in ecclesiastical dress. His henchmen, including some monks, torture a man on a table until he vomits money. A fleece of a sheep is hanging on the wall while a shorn lamb walks on the floor.

XIII The End: Ascent or Descent (D3v–D4r)

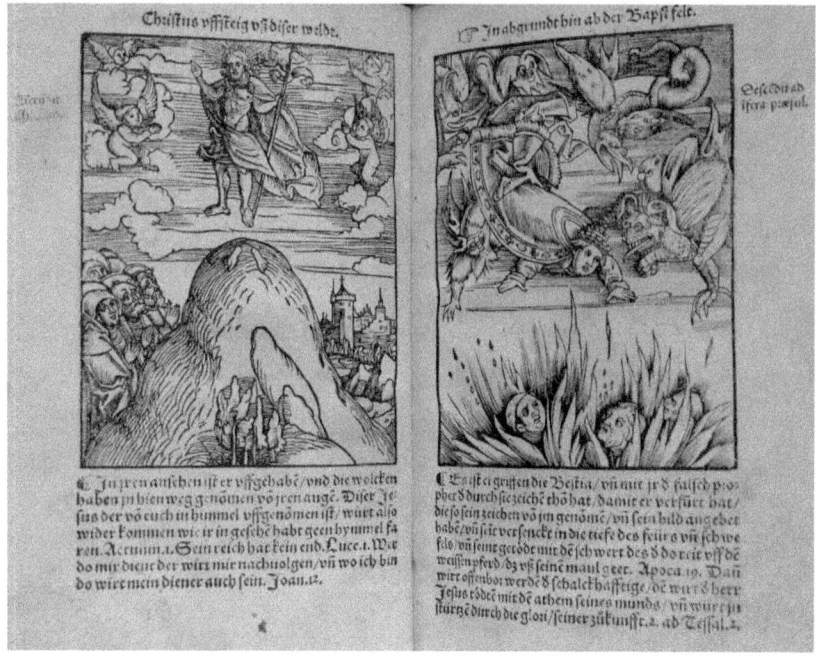

Christus vffsteig vß diser weldt. ☞ Jn abgrundt hin ab der Bapst felt.

Ascendit Christus. Descendit ad infera præsul.

Translation

Christ ascended from this world. The pope falls down into the depths.

Christ ascends. The bishop descends to hell.

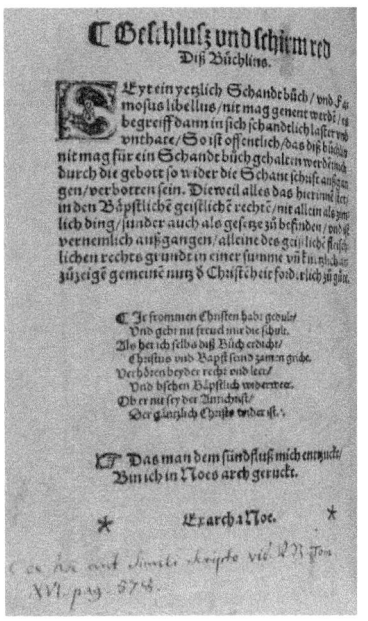

Postscript (D2v)

Beschlusz vnd schirm red Diß Bůchlins.

Jr frommen Christen habt gedult/
Vnd gebt nit freuel mir die schult.
Als het ich selbs diß Bůch erdicht/
Christus vnd Bapst seind zamen gricht.
Verhören beyder recht vnd leer/
Vnd bsehen Båpstlich widerweer.
Ob er nit sey der Antichrist/
Der gåntzlich Christo wider ist.

☞ Das man dem sündfluß mich enttzuckt/
Bin ich in Noes arch geruckt.

* Ex archa Noe. *

Translation

Conclusion and defence of this little book.

You pious Christians have patience,
And do not blame me for this outrage.
As if I myself have composed this book,
That Christ and the pope are brought together.
Examine both through law and teaching,
Observe the papal reply.
Whether he is not the Antichrist
Who is completely in opposition to Christ.
So that I may be snatched from the Great Flood,
I have been put[162] in Noah's ark.
From the ark of Noah.

---

[162] Text according to the Taylorian copy. WA 9, 715 has the pun *getruckt* which can mean 'printed' as well as 'squeezed' instead of *geruckt* which can only mean 'put'.

3. Facsimile of the German edition

Erfurt 1521, Taylorian, ARCH.8°.G.1521(19)

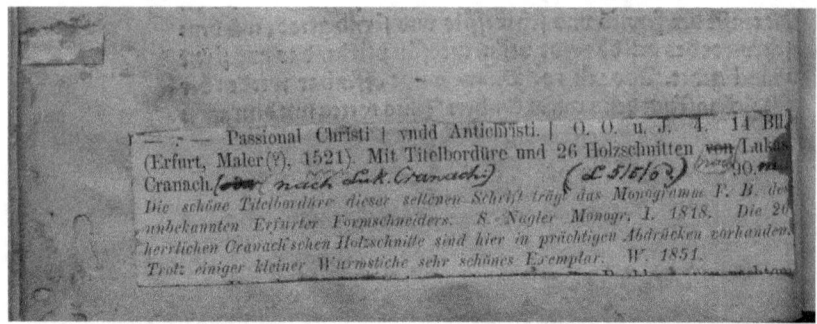

Glued in entry for the Taylorian copy from the German auction catalogue, praising the "beautiful copy despite some worm holes", some of which are visible on the left, together with an old tab, indicating it was part of a 'Sammelband'.

Titlepage: Passional of Christ and Antichrist, monogram FB, date 1521

Paſſional Chꝛiſti vnd

Chꝛiſtus.

Do Jheſus innen wardt/das ſie kommen wurden vnd yhnen
zum köníg machen/iſt er abermals vffin bergk geflohen/er al¬
lein. Johan. 6. Mein reich iſt nicht võ diſzer welt. Joh. 18. Die
könnige der welt hirſchen yr/vnnd die gewaldt haben/werden
gnedige hern genandt/yr aber nicht alſzo/ſonder der do groſſer
iſt vnther euch/ſall ſich nydern/als der weniger. Luce. zz.

I 1: Christ refuses the crown (A1v)

Antichzisti.

Antichzistus.

Auß oburkayt die wir sonder zweiffell zum keysserthüb haben/
vnd auß vnser gewalt/ seynt wir des keysertumbs/ so sich das
vozledigt/ein rechter erbe.cle.pastozalis ad si. de sen.et re.indi.
Süma summarū.Nichts anders ist in des Bapsts geystlichē
rechte zu finden/dan das es seynen abgot vnd Antichzist vbir
alle keysser/könig vñ fursten yrhebet/als Petrus vozgesagt hat.
Es werden kōmen vnuozschambte Bischoff die die weltlich
herschafft werden vozachten.z.Pet.z.   A ij

I 2: The pope accepts the crown (A2r)

Paſſional Chriſti vnd

Chriſtus.
Die ſoldner haben gefloch ten eyne kronen von dörnen / vñ auff
ſein heubt gedꝛuckt/darnach mit eynem purper kleydt haben ſie
yn bekleydet   Johan.19.

II 3: Christ is crowned with thorns (A2v)

Antichriſti.

Antichriſtus.

Der Keyſer Conſtantinus hat vns die keyſerlich krone/ getzirde
allen andern geſchmuck in maſſen wie yhn d keyſer tregt / purper cleyt alle andere cleyder vñ ſcepter zutragen vñ zubzauchen
geben. c. Conſtantinus. cxvi. diſ. Solche lügen haben ſie yre tr-
ranney zu erhalten ertichtwyder alle hiſtouen vñ kuntſchaffe
dan es iſt nit brauchlich geweßen den Romiſchen Keyſern ein
ſolche krone zutragen.   A iij

II 4: The pope is crowned with a tiara (A3r)

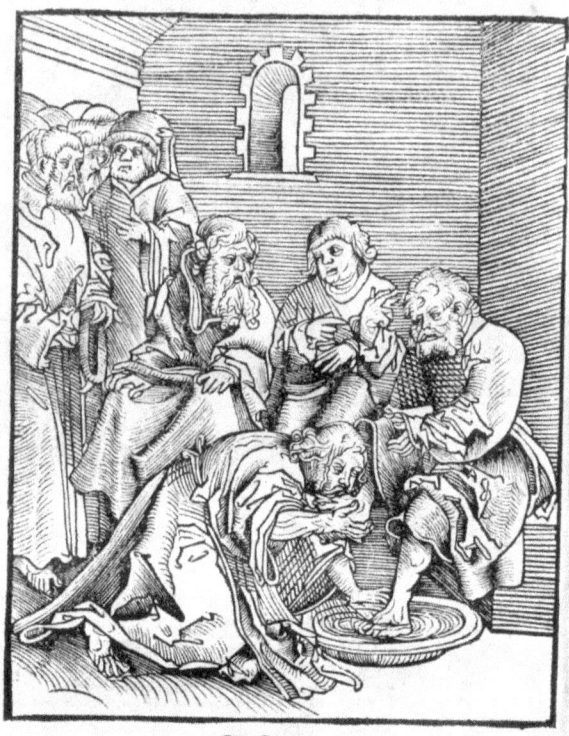

Paſſional Chꝛiſti vnd

Chꝛiſtus.

Szo ich ewꝛe fueſze habe gewaſchen ð ich ewir herꝛ vñ meyſter
bin/vill mehꝛ ſolt yr einander vnter euch die fuſze waſchen. Hie/
mit habe ich euch ein anzeygung vñ beyſpiel geben/ wie ich ym
than habe / alſzo ſolt yr hinfur auch thuen. Warlich warlich
ſage ich euch/ð knecht iſt nicht mehꝛ dan ſeyn herꝛe/ ſzo iſt auch
nicht ð geſchickte botte mehꝛ dā ð yn geſandt hat/Wiſt yr das!
Selig ſeyt yr ſzo yr das thuen werden̄t. Johan.13.

III 5: Christ washes the disciples' feet (A3v)

Antichristi.

Antichristus.

Der Babst maßt sich an iglichen Tyrannen vnd heydnischen
fursten/ßo yre fueß den leuten zu kussen dar gereicht/ nach zu
volgen/damit es waer werde das geschriben ist.Wilcher dieser
bestien bilde nicht anbettet/ sall getöd werden. Apocalip.13.
Diß kussens darff sich der Bapst vn seynē decretaun vnuor
schembt rümen.c.cū oli dē pri.cle. Si summus pon.de sen.exes.

III 6: The pope has his feet kissed (A4r)

Paſſional Chꝛiſti vnd

Chꝛiſtus.

Gehe hyn zum meh꞉/vñ laß yn dynen hamen/ dem erſten fiſch
der ſich vff wirfft/thue das mauel auff/ doꝛinnen wirſtu findē
einen gulden/den gib zu zoll voꝛ mich vnd dich. Math. 17
Gebt der obirkeyt die das ſchwerdt in yren henden hat ſeyne ge
büre/den zinß/wem der zinß zuſtehet/den zoll deꝫ er gebürdt.
Paul.ad Roma. 13.

IV 7: Christ and Peter pay customs (A4v)

Antichristi.

Wir setzen vnd ordnen das den mit nicht gezimen sall so den
weltlichen gerichts gwägk habe stewir vñ schoß dē geystlichen
personen vffzulegen ader den zu foderen von yren hewsirn vñ
allen andern guttern bey der puß des schweren bans vnd inter-
dictis / des gleychen sollen die geystlichen dieße alle nicht zalen
sonder vnßer erleubnis .c.1.de imunit. eccle.li.vi. Also h it der
Babst gots gebot durch seyne gebott zurissen / welchs seyner
vnchristlichen decretael eynigs werck ist.   B

IV 8: The pope stops taxation of the clergy (B1r)

Paſſional Chꝛiſti vnd

Chꝛiſtus.

Chꝛiſtus aber wol yn der gotlichen foꝛm war/ bennoch hat er
ſich des geewſert ſich genydert vñ geberdet wie ein knecht gleich
den andern menſchen an zuſehen vnd befunden ein menſch der
ſich gedmütiget hatt/ vnnd iſt gehoꝛſam geweſen biß in den
todt. Philippenſes. z.

V 9: Christ prays with the lame, lepers and blind (B1v)

Antichꝛiſti.

Antichꝛiſtus.

Der Bapſt meynt eꝫ ſey ſeynen ehꝛen ʒu nahe das er ſich demů
tige / dan der ſich ʒu faſt demůtiget gedeyet yhm yn dem regi
ment ʒuuoꝛachtung.c.quando 86.diſt.

Alſo ſagt die gloſa / das iſt waer bey den narren / das iſt ßo vill
man muß geſtreng vbir die deutſchen narren regiren / ſo halten
ſie veil von vns.   B ij

V 10: The pope presides over a knight's tournament (B2r)

Paſſional Chriſti vnd

Chriſtus.

Alß Jheſus iſt eyn weytten wegk gangen / iſt er müd worden.
Johan. 4. Der mir will nach folgen / der nem ſeyn Creutz vff
ſich vnd folge mir. Matthei 16.
Er hat ym ſeyn Creutze ſelbeſt getragen vnd iſt zu der ſtell die
Caluarie genant wirdt / gangen. 19.

VI 11: Christ carries his cross (B2v)

Antichꝛiſti.

Antichꝛiſtus.

Das capittel Si quis ſuadente vñ der gleychen zeygt gnug an
wie gerne der Bapſt das Creutz der wyderwertigkeyt duldet/ſo
er alle die ihenen/die handt an die pfaffen an legē voꝛmaladeyet
vñ dem teuffel gibt Vnd alßo ouch tregt der Bapſt das Creutz
das ynnen getauffte Chꝛiſten uff yren achſſelen tragen muſſen.
B iij

VI 12: The pope is carried on a palanquin (B3r)

Paſſional Chriſti und

Chriſtus.
Ich muß auch andern ſteten predigen das reych gots/dan ich von deß wegen geſandt byn / vnd hab gepredigt in den Sina⸗ gogen durch Galileam Luce. 4.

VII 13: Christ preaches to the people (B3v)

Antichristi.

Es geschicht offt das die Bischoff mit vielen hendlen beladen
seyn/ vnd von wegen yrer fheden/ auch zun zeytten konnen sies
nit/ das dan mit seyn soll/ mögen des predigens nit gewarten/
sonderlich wan yre bißtumb groß seint/ dann mögen sie andere
vor sich bestellen/ die do predigen.c. Inter cetera de offi. ordina.
Das seynd die bischoff die yres ordenlichen ampts vergessen/ sint
worden amaha vdris. vñ sprechen/ kümet vñ last vns schlemen
z mit temmen vnd also far vnd far güt leben haben. Esai. 56.

VII 14: The pope at a feast (B4r)

Paſſional Chriſti vnd

Chriſtus

Die füchß haben yre gruben / vnd die fogell der lufft yre neſter/
Aber d̕ ſon des menſchen hat nicht do er ſeyn heubt legte. Lu. 9.
Dieſſer ab er woll reich war / dennoch vmb vnſert willen iſt er
arm woꝛden/vnd ſeyn armut hat vns reich gemacht. 2. Coꝛ. 8.

VIII 15: Birth of Christ in the stable (B4v)

Antichristi.

Wir loßen auff alle eyde die die geyſtlichen zu gefengknis gelo=
bet haben vnnd gebieten das mann nit allein mit geyſtlichem/
ſonder auch mit dem weltlichem ſchwerdt yre gütter beſchutzē
ſall/ſo lang biß das ſie yr etwandt gutt widder haben 15.q. 6
c. Auctoritatem/vnd der yn dieſem krieck ſtirbt adir vordirbet
wirt erlangen das ewig leben 23.q.5.c. Oim et q.8.c. Omni/
das heyſt ſeyns guts gewiß ſein/das mans auch vor gut acht.
ob ſchon chriſten blůt daruber vorgoſſen wirdt.   C

VIII 16: The pope wages war (C1r)

Paſſional Chꝛiſti vnd

Chꝛiſtus.

Sich an/ dein konigk kompt dir demütigk vff einen iungen eſ
Mathei z ı. Alſo iſt Chꝛiſtus kommen reyttende vffinn frembꝛ
den eſel arm vnd ſanfftmütigk vnd reydt nicht zu regiren ſonꝛ
der vns allen zu eynem ſeligen todte Johannis ız.

IX 17: Christ rides into Jerusalem on a donkey (C1v)

Antichristi.

Antichristi.

Die geystlichen seindt alle könnige vnd das bezeygt die platten vff im kopffe. Duo iz. q.i.

Der Bapst magk gleich wie der keysser reytten vnd der keyser ist seyn thrabant vff das bischofflicher wirdē gehalt nicht gemindert werde. c. Constantinus. 96. dis.

Der Bapst ist allen volckern vñ reychen vorgesatzt er. vag. sup. gentes. Johannis zz.   C ij

IX 18: The pope rides into hell on a steed (C2r)

Paſſional Chriſti vnd

Chriſtus
Ir ſolt nicht haben golt nach ſilber/nicht gelt an ewirn gortelñ
keyne taſchen auch nit zwen rock noch ſchuch/nach eyn wan/
berſtab.Math.10.
Sanct peter ſagt/Ich habe wyder golt nach ſilber Act. 3 ª
Obi iſt dan patrimonium petri

X 19: Christ sends out the disciples (C2v)

Antichꝛisti.

Antichꝛistus

Eyn Biſchoff ſall auff eyn gering vnd kleyne ſtadt gꝛweret
ro iden/ ſondern zu eynem erlichen Titell geſatzt vnd hoch geꝛ
ehꝛet ſeyn . 80. diſt c. Epiſcopi.

Wir oꝛdnen das keyne werhung ane gnugliche voꝛſoꝛgiꝛg
treffag ſey. 70. diſt. ſanctoꝛum.   C iij

X 20: The pope shows a bishop a castle (C3r)

Passional Christi vnd

Christus.

Das reich gots ist nit yn ewsserlichen geberden/sie hie / aber do
ist Christus / besonder das reich gots ist innerlich in euch. Lu.
17. Warumb habt ir das gebott gots vbirtretten võ menschē
gesetz wegenn/ Alle ehren mich vorgeblich / die do menschen lere
vnnd gebott halten. Mat. 15. Esaie. 21.

XI 21: Christ argues with the Pharisees (C3v)

Antichriſt.

Des Antichriſts reich iſt gantzlich in erꝛßerlichem weſen/
was ſagt des Bapſts recht anders den oꝛdnung/ von kaſeln/
cleydern/plattẽ/feyertagẽ/weyungẽ/pfreunden/ſectẽ/monchen
vnd pfaffen/ vñ nennen ſich/yr habe vnd gutter geyſtlich gutt/
ſich allein die Chꝛiſtlich kirche / die pfaffen dz außerwelt volck
gots/gleich ſam weren die leyen nicht in der kirchen vnd gots/
widder alle ſchꝛifft/ vbir das verbeut er die ſpeyße/ ehe/wie dan
Paulus voꝛgeſagt hat. Es werden kōmen voꝛlogne geyſt/ vnd
ſolche ding voꝛbieten. 1. Timo. 4.

XI 22: The pope is worshipped by clergy and people (C4r)

Paſſional Chꝛiſti vnd

Er hat funden ym tẽpel voꝛkauffer/ſchaff/ochſſen vñ tawben
vñ wechſler ſitzen/vñ hat gleich eyn geyſſel gemacht võ ſtrickl
alle ſchaff/ochſſen/ taubẽ vñ wechßler auſſem tempell triben/
das gelt verſchüt/ die ꝗall bꝛedt vmkart vñ ꝗu den die tawben
voꝛkauffcen geſpꝛochen. Hebt euch hin mit dieſſen auß meine
vatern hauß/ſolt ir nit ein kauffhauß machẽ. Joh.z. Jr habts
vmb ſunſt/daꝛüb gebts vmb ſunſt. Mat.19. Dein gelt ſey mit
dir yn voꝛdammuß. Act.8

XII 23: Christ drives out the money changers from the temple (C4v)

Antichristi.

Hie sitzt der Antichrist ym tempell gots vnd erzeygt sich als got
wie Paulus vorkundet. z. Tessal. z. vorandert alle gotlich ordnung / wie Daniel sagt / vnnd vnterdruckt die heylig schrifft/
vorkeufft dispensacion/Ablas/Pallia/Bisthum/Lehen/erhebt
die schetz der erden/lost auff die ehe/beschwerdt die gewissen mit
seynen gesetzen / macht recht / vnnd vmb gelt zureyst er das/
Erhebt heyligen/benedeyet vn maledeyet yns vierde geschlecht
vnd gebewt sein stym zuhoren/gleych wie gots stym.c. sic ois.
dist.19.vnd niemants sall ym eynreden.17.q.4.c. Nemini.
D

XII 24: The pope sits in church, selling sealed letters (D1r)

Paſſional Chriſti vnd

Jn yren anſehen iſt er auffgehaben vnd die wolcken haben ynn hinwegk genomenn vō yren ougen. Diſer Jeſus der von euch yn himmel auffgenommen iſt/ wirde alſo wyder kommen wie yr ynn geſehen habt zu himmel fharen. Act. 1. Seyn reych haß keyn ende Luce. 1. Wer do mir dient der wird mir nach volgen vñ wu ich bin do wirt meyn diener ouch ſeyn Johā. 12.

XIII 25: Christ ascends to heaven (D1v)

Antlchriſtl.

Es iſt ergriffen die Beſtia vñ mit yr d̄ falſchpropheet der durch
ſie zeychen than hat/do mit er vorfurdt hat/die ſo ſeyn zeychē
von ym genommen / vnd ſein bildt angebet ſeynt verſenckt yn
die teuffe des fewirs vnd ſchweffels vnd ſeynd getodt mit dem
ſchwerdt des der do reydt vffim weyſſen pferdt/ das auß ſeynē
mauel gehet. Apocal: 19. Danne wirdt offenbar werden der
ſchalckhafftige denn wirdt der herr Jeſus toeten mit dem atem
ſeyns mundts vnd wirdt yn ſturtzen durch die glori ſeyner zu
kunfft. z. ad Teſſa .z.   D ij

XIII 26: The pope descends to hell (D2r)

¶ Sint eyn itzlich schandt buch/vnd famosus libellus nit mag
genendt werden/es begreyfft dan yn sich schandtlich laster vnd
vnthate/ßo ist offentlich / dz ditz buchle nit mag vor ein schade
buch gehalte werde/nach durch die gebot so widder die schad
schufft auß gangen /vorbotten sein/ dieweyl alles das hirinnen
steht/yn dem Bepstlichem geysiliche rechte/ nit allein als zimi
lich dinge / sonder auch als gesetze tzubesinden / vnnd ist vor
nemlich außgägen/ alleine deß geystlichen/ fleyschlichen rechts
grundt yn eyner summe vnnd kurtzlich antzutzeygen gemeynem
nutz der Christenheyt forderlich tzu gutte.

¶ Nembt allßo vor gutte/
Es wirt baldt besser werden.

Passional Christi | vndd Antichristi. | O. O. u. J. 14 Bll.
(Erfurt, Maler(?), 1521). Mit Titelbordüre und 26 Holzschnitten von Lukas
Cranach.
Die schöne Titelbordüre dieser seltenen Schrift trägt das Monogramm L. B. des
unbekannten Erfurter Formschneiders. S. Nagler Monogr. I. 1818. Die 26
herrlichen Cranach'schen Holzschnitte sind hier in prächtigen Abdrücken vorhanden.
Trotz einiger kleiner Wurmstiche sehr schönes Exemplar. W. 1851.

Postscript (D2v)